SWEDISH HANDKNITS

A COLLECTION OF HEIRLOOM DESIGNS

SUE FLANDERS AND JANINE KOSEL

Foreword by Nina Clark and Curt Pederson of the American Swedish Institute

Voyageur Press

First published in 2012 by Voyageur Press, an imprint of MBI Publishing Company, 400 First Avenue North, Suite 300, Minneapolis, MN 55401 USA

Voyageur Press titles are also available at discounts in bulk quantity for industrial or sales-promotional use. For details write to Special Sales Manager at MBI Publishing Company, 400 First Avenue North, Suite 300, Minneapolis, MN 55401 USA.

To find out more about our books,
visit us online at www.voyageurpress.com.

ISBN-13: 978-0-7603-3964-0

Editor: Kari Cornell
Design Manager: Cindy Samargia Laun
Cover Designer: Ellen Huber

Library of Congress Cataloging-in-Publication Data

Flanders, Sue, 1960–
  Swedish handknits : a collection of heirloom designs / Sue Flanders and Janine Kosel ; foreword by Curt Pederson and Nina Clark, American Swedish Institute.
    ISBN 978-0-7603-3964-0 (hardback)
  1. Knitting--Patterns. 2. Knitting--Sweden. I. Kosel, Janine, 1964– II. Title.
  TT825.F557 2012
  746.43'2--dc23
                2012005913

We dedicate this book to a few of the knitting and fiber world's greatest teachers and designers, from whom we have learned so very much: Sidna Farly, Joyce Williams, Ann Swanson, Syvilla Bolson, and Elizabeth Zimmermann.

On the frontispiece:
The Twined Knit Christmas Sock, Tree motif, in progress.

On the title page:
Anna Neils with knitting, circa 1910.
MINNESOTA HISTORICAL SOCIETY COLLECTION

Contents

Foreword

by Nina Clark and Curt Pederson of the American Swedish Institute

This book, *Swedish Handknits: A Collection of Heirloom Designs*, has as many layers as a warm bed on a cold winter's night. Authors Sue Flanders and Janine Kosel have artfully investigated the collections and environs of the American Swedish Institute (ASI) in Minneapolis, Minnesota, to divine inspiration and create new life from old motifs. Through the patterns that appear on these pages, Sue and Janine honor the handiwork of artists and artisans of years past while perpetuating their creativity and dedication. And with this book, they are cultivating a circle of followers who will gather around these patterns with joyful, busy hands— just as generations have gathered at the American Swedish Institute to care for this old mansion and serve untold cups of coffee, in companionship. Below is what we can share of their sources for inspiration.

An Introduction to the American Swedish Institute

The American Swedish Institute in Minneapolis is an organization with a long memory and enduring community, tied up in the culture and craft of the Swedish Americans who have steered and supported it for more than eighty years. The institute was founded by a Swedish immigrant family who imagined an organization that would serve as a center for Swedish culture in the United States, and it stands true to that original vision today. But it is also a gathering place that invites and welcomes people of all backgrounds, interested in craft, the arts, migration, and the history of Minneapolis and Minnesota.

Swan Turnblad family – Swan J., his wife, Christina, and their daughter, Lillian.
AMERICAN SWEDISH INSTITUTE COLLECTION

Left: The American Swedish Institute at dawn, 2010.

The Turnblads

In 1868, eight-year-old Sven Johan Månsson left Sweden with his mother, father, sister, and brother. According to the ship's manifest, he landed in New York City as Swan J. Turnblad. This man, who would come to establish the American Swedish Institute with his wife, Christina, and daughter, Lillian, came to the United States during the peak years for emigration from Sweden—the so called "bark-bread years," when meager grain supplies drove families to supplement flour with ground bark. In all, over one million people left Sweden for the United States from the 1850s to the 1940s. Swan's immediate family followed other Månssons, who also changed their names to Turnblad before continuing on to Vasa in Goodhue County, Minnesota. Swan's early interest in printing eventually put him on the road to Minneapolis, where in time he became owner of the largest Swedish language newspaper in the United States, the *Svenska Amerikanska Posten*. He met Christina Nilsson at a temperance dance; they married and had one daughter, Lillian Zenobia. Swan, an automobile enthusiast, purchased land on the city's first asphalt-paved street—Park Avenue. On these six city lots, the Turnblads had their mansion built.

The Mansion

Completed in 1908, the Turnblads' thirty-three room mansion is a tribute to the craftsmanship that was then both remarkable and commonplace. Like many well-to-do people of their time, the Turnblads passed many summers in Europe and gathered ideas—even pattern books—that offered inspiration for their interiors. The house's two-story Grand Hall is distinguished by an ornately carved mahogany mantel. From any vantage point in the Hall, one can view the Visby Window, a stained-glass window depicting a classic painting in Sweden's National Museum. The decorations that adorn the plaster ceilings throughout the mansion bring to mind wedding cakes covered with elaborately piped frosting. And eleven different tile stoves—*kakelugnar* in Swedish—imported from Sweden offer new discoveries at the second, third, and fourth look. In 1908, Prairie School architecture was coming on strong, but the Turnblads' sensibilities embraced Old Europe. Lucky for us—it's the variety of detail, inside and out, that has offered inspiration for some of the patterns in this book.

The Founding of the ASI

In 1929, after Christina Turnblad passed away, Swan and Lillian established what was initially called the American Institute of Swedish Arts, Literature, and Science, later renamed the American Swedish Institute. When the institute first opened, people streamed in to see the fantastic residence. Turnblad had envisioned the institute as a high-culture, erudite organization led by a national board of business and civic leaders. But these individuals weren't vested, and activities faltered. The mansion did not stay quiet for long. Swedes of all stripes recognized that the building was an excellent place to gather, and soon social and service clubs moved in to hold meetings, celebrations, and presentations. What had been the home for one family rapidly became a second home for an entire community. The "Institute" was such in name only, and those expecting a quiet, scholarly enterprise would be surprised. Pride in this special place multiplied and grew, and the castle that offered shelter was cared for in return.

Women on a country road near Hällberg, Dalarne, Sweden, August 1, 1914.
AMERICAN SWEDISH INSTITUTE COLLECTION

The Collections

From the ASI's earliest days, items were accrued for the collection. Over the years, the library, which began with books the Turnblads had collected during trips back to Sweden, grew with donations of more books, diaries, letters, photos, recordings, club records, and other items. At the same time, Swedish American families donated artifacts representing every imaginable item that may have been carried from Sweden to America by émigrés. Over the years, the American Swedish Institute has actively collected contemporary Swedish glass, and the institute is home to the nation's largest collection of Swedish figure carvings—more than six hundred in total. A high point in the history of the collection was the donation of the Värmland Gift in 1952. As a collective token of the friendship between the two lands, every parish in the province of Värmland donated items to be sent to the American Swedish Institute.

Herr and Fru Petterson and family at Summermäla, Elmeboda, Sweden, August 19, 1914.
AMERICAN SWEDISH INSTITUTE COLLECTION

Textiles in Sweden and Swedish America

Swedish textile crafts, including bed coverlets, loom-woven rugs, tablecloths, and runners, are particularly rewarding to study due to a wealth of accessible historical examples in both Sweden and Swedish America. In some areas of Sweden, successive craft traditions have never been broken, spanning centuries of transition from agrarian society to today's twenty-first-century technology. When 1800s industrialization consumed manpower from traditional households, Swedish textile crafts were generally those that survived. The Handcraft Movement, a reaction to extensive industrial production, redirected attention to home craft production. Textile crafts like loom-woven linen and rugs, spinning, embroidery, and knitting played an important role in the birth of the Handcraft Movement and remain among the strongest practiced handcraft traditions today in Sweden.

When Swedish immigrants came to America, they brought tools and knowledge of practices that provided linens and domestic textiles for families of settlers throughout the Midwest. The descendants of these immigrants have been instrumental in building the fiber collections at the American Swedish Institute. Today the collection exists as an historic record, but is equally important as a source of inspiration for twenty-first-century scholars and artists, which is exactly what Swedish immigrant Swan Turnblad envisioned when he established the American Swedish Institute.

The textile collection includes examples of traditional Swedish weave types, motifs, materials, and natural and commercially made dyes used during the immigration period. The patterns found on bed coverlets, pillows, runners, garments, and Swedish provincial costumes are sources of inspiration for the patterns in this book. The pieces reveal how Swedish traditions were continued in this country and how those traditions influenced textiles more generally in the Midwest.

The Larsson/Lundin Family

The ASI collection includes a trunk, spinning wheel, wood bench—"Drag-Sossa"—loom, and textiles woven by Anna Olsdotter Lundin. Descendents of Anna and her husband, Lars Larsson, were inspired by the couple's great-granddaughter, Tess Henry, to donate these family heirlooms to the American Swedish Institute. This is the largest material collection from any single immigrant family in the collection. A written history of Lars and Anna and their descendents to this century accompanies the donation:

Fru Anna Anderson in her home at Billa, Sweden, June 1914. Notice the woven rugs on the floor.
AMERICAN SWEDISH INSTITUTE COLLECTION

Lars Larsson and his wife, Anna Olsdotter Lundin, were Swedish immigrants who came to central Minnesota with a wood handmade trunk that bore its maker's name and destination, "L. Larsson/Cokato Minnesota, North Amerika." Lars and Anna cut trees and built a small log cabin. Next, using trees on their land, Lars built a loom and Anna rigged the warp for weaving, as she had learned in Sweden. Tess Henry's memories of her great-grandmother, Anna, include smoking a pipe filled with her home-grown tobacco and the annual fall ritual of laying clean straw on the wood floor of the farmhouse, covering it with Anna's beautiful woven rugs for insulation. This wall-to-wall carpet would stay in place until spring when the rugs would be taken up, the straw swept up and the floors washed.

Legendary Textile Figures

In addition to the textiles used on a day-to-day basis in immigrant homes, the textile collection also includes the work of Swedish textile giants Märta Måås-Fjetterström and Helena Hernmarck. At a time when most rugs in Sweden were simple rag rugs, careful study of the Swedish countryside led artist Märta Mååjs Fjetterström (1873–1941) to design and produce rugs of high quality that reflected Swedish cultural traditions. Her carpets have been featured in exhibitions all over the world.

A master weaver, Helena Hernmarck's work encapsulates traditions and the outdoors in heroic scale. Her work has been selected for scores of public spaces and enjoyed by millions of viewers. In 2004, Helena was inspired by the folk textile collection at the ASI and was commissioned to create a 10x15-foot tapestry depicting the colorful woven and stitched elements of Swedish folk costumes from the collection. The tapestry hangs in ASI's Nelson Cultural Center.

But if there's a patron saint of textiles at ASI, it must be Hilma Berglund. Hilma Berglund studied weaving in Sweden and was a lifelong student, teacher, and innovator in textile and other arts. Countless accomplishments included extensive documentation of experiments using natural dyes on a variety of fibers, and design and manufacture of "the Minnesota loom," portable for instruction anywhere. Hilma left a lasting legacy as one of the founders of the Minnesota Weavers Guild and as a dedicated University of Minnesota teacher of weaving.

One of Hilma's weavings from the collection intertwines the shape of Minnesota's state flower, the Lady Slipper, to form a rectangular vertical wall hanging, using colors for the fall season. To make the Lady Slipper tapestry, Hilma used an inlay technique that she likely learned while studying weaving at a handcraft school in Stockholm, Sweden.

Coming Together around Knitting

True to the spirit of this community, knitting is a social act—in the passing down of the craft, the doing together, and the sharing of the creative goods. This is what ASI has been engaged in since 1929—respect for history, working together, and sharing in celebrations and creative, cultural pursuits. In 2009, the exhibit *Radiant Knits* celebrated the Bohus knitting tradition, bringing together pieces from all over the United States and attracting knitters from far and wide for "knit-outs" in the mansion. At ASI, artistry and community are hand in hand.

For this reason, ASI staff and volunteers feel lucky to be an audience to the shaping of *Swedish Handknits*. The inspiration found on these pages has given new interest and life to the ASI collection. We began to anticipate the next visit from authors Sue Flanders and Janine Kosel, wondering what they would create next. While they studied ASI's textile collection, we were delighted at their attention to what is referred to as "the largest piece in the collection," the mansion "castle" itself. They drew inspiration from architectural details or repeated decorative motifs. We were sometimes surprised to witness Sue and Janine's excitement at the smallest detail, like an embroidered motif on a Swedish embroidered table linen. On their next visit to ASI, sometimes as soon as the next day, these knitters/authors had already translated the detail into an actual knit piece.

How exciting to see a motif gleaned from an old piece, reinterpreted, sometimes in a different color, size, or perspective. One feels that our founders, the Turnblad family, would be smiling with delight—not overly joyous, of course, but with proper Nordic restraint.

Using boards from her father's lumber yard, Hilma fabricated the first "Minnesota Multi-Use Loom" after World War II (it was produced until the early 1970s). This loom, designed to permit two or more weavers to work on their individual pieces interchangeably, was used extensively to provide occupational therapy to World War II veterans as they recovered from injuries. The loom is a four-shaft, 20-inch-wide jack (rising shed) table loom. A stand, with four treadles connecting to the hand levers, converts the table loom into a foot-powered loom. The heddle frames, reed, warp, and cloth beams can be removed and stored with the holding rack provided, allowing another set to be installed in the loom frame. AMERICAN SWEDISH INSTITUTE COLLECTION

Introduction

For us, the research for *Swedish Handknits: A Collection of Heirloom Designs* began years ago. As young girls, we each remember our first trip to the American Swedish Institute—crossing the threshold of the iron gates and peering up at the mansion was a magical experience. We were certain that a beautiful princess lived in this castle, and we could hardly believe that we would be allowed inside. With our mothers holding tight to our hands to keep us from touching anything, we looked with wide eyes and curious minds. While on the mansion tour, we took in its many beautiful sights—the porcelain stoves, the woodwork, the carpets, the staircases, the textiles, and the paintings. These first trips to the ASI left a lasting impression on both of us. Little did we know as young girls that years later our memories would be the foundation for this book you hold in your hands.

A few years ago, while on a trip to Norway and Sweden, we gathered momentum for this project. While in Sweden, we visited a number of textile museums, including the Jamtli museum in Ostersund, the Dalarnas Museum in Falun, and the Nordiska Museet in Stockholm. During these visits, we learned of the extensive Swedish textile traditions. Being impressed by the variety of knitting techniques and styles, we thought it was important to write a book that gathered all of these Swedish knitting traditions under one cover.

In this collection of patterns, our follow-up to *Norwegian Handknits: Heirloom Designs from Vesterheim Museum*, we followed the same book concept, including personal histories, recipes, and bits of Swedish folklore and culture along with the knitting patterns. We have used elements of traditional immigrant items and Swedish American–made items, such as weavings, paintings, and other handwork, as inspiration. It is interesting to note that the ASI mission statement gives a well-deserved nod to the contributions of Swedish immigrants, yet has an eye on contemporary Sweden as well. In fact, one of the special exhibits we viewed during our research showcased work from modern Swedish women interior designers.

We have included regional knitting traditions such as the Swedish Mittens, made on the Island of Gotland, twined knitting from the Darlana area of Sweden, and the more famous Swedish knitting traditions of the Bohus knitting cooperative. In some cases, we have modified techniques to honor knitters who have come before us, and in other cases, we have created some of our own techniques.

So, from the big eyes of young girls to the grand ideas of two overwhelmed knitters, we present *Swedish Handknits: A Collection of Heirloom Designs*.

A rustic Swedish gate at Jamtli Museum, Sweden.

Opposite: Girls in costume at Rättvik, Sweden, August 2, 1914. AMERICAN SWEDISH INSTITUTE COLLECTION

CHAPTER 1

Basic Knitting Techniques

Farbror Johan, Gösta, Faster Ingrid at Westragård, August 18, 1914.
AMERICAN SWEDISH INSTITUTE COLLECTION

Although these designs are basic in nature, completing them provides the satisfaction of a hearty, useful item worthy of a busy woman's time and a project well done. These items are examples of what a busy pioneer, immigrant woman may have knit for her family after first attending to numerous other chores. Notice the use of color and the simple beauty in each of these items.

Everyday Leggings

Size
Adult's Average

Finished Measurements
Circumference: 8"/20.5cm at
ankle; 10"/25.5cm at knee
Length: 16"/40.5cm

Materials

- Classy by Dream in Color
  Yarns, 100% Merino wool,
  100g/3.5oz, 250yds/229m:
- Cinnamon Girl #VM 011
  (MC) and Romeo Blue #VM
  007 (CC), 1 skein each
- Size 8 (5mm) 24"/61cm
  long circular needle or size
  needed to obtain gauge
- Size 7 (4.5mm) 16"/40.5cm
  long circular needle
- Waste yarn
- Tapestry needle

Gauge
18 sts and 10 rows = 4"/10cm
in Garter st on larger needle.
Adjust needle size as necessary to obtain correct gauge.

We found these well-used, well-loved leggings in a beautiful built-in drawer in a storage room at the American Swedish Institute. We loved these simple but oh-so-wonderful leggings as soon as we saw them. In keeping with our goal to also feature an everyday item, we've given these leggings a bit of an update. It really is true: everything old is new again!

Special Techniques
Provisional Cast-On (see Special Techniques Used, page 140)

Instructions

LEGGINGS (MAKE 2)
With waste yarn, using provisional cast-on method, CO 75 sts.
Row 1: With MC and larger needle k50, cont with MC and smaller needle k25. Turn.

Row 2: Cont with MC and smaller needle k25, cont with MC and larger needle k50. Turn.

Row 3: With CC and larger needle k50, cont with CC and smaller needle k25. Turn.

Row 4: Cont with CC and smaller needle k25, cont with CC and larger needle k50. Turn.

Rep Rows 1–4 until there are 24 MC ridges and 23 CC ridges.

Cut off MC, leaving a 4"/10cm tail to weave in.

Next: Using CC and larger needle only, k75 sts.

Unzip provisional cast-on placing live sts on smaller needle.

FINISHING

Close seam with Kitchener stitch in Garter st as foll:

Cut a length of CC approx. 1 yard long. Thread this end onto tapestry needle. With WSs together and holding the circular needles parallel so that the 1-yard length is coming out of the needle in the back, begin to rep the foll two steps across your work:

Step 1: On front needle, with tapestry needle, go into first st as if to knit and take it off left needle; go into second st on left needle as if to purl and leave it on left needle; draw thread through.

Step 2: On back needle, with tapestry needle, go into first st as if to knit and take it off left needle; go into second st on left needle as if to purl and leave it on left needle; draw thread through.

Note: To better understand where you are in the Kitchener stitch pat, these directions have you do the work on your tapestry needle. Keep tension of each pull as even as you can with the tension of your knitting. Weave in ends.

These basic crocheted, utilitarian leggings from the American Swedish Institute textile collection were the inspiration for our Everyday Leggings design.

Long Stocking Hat

Size
Adult's Average

Finished Measurements
Circumference: 20"/51cm
Height: 45"/114.5cm (from top to tip)

Materials

- Hand-Dyed Montana Merino by Ewetopian Fibers, 100% wool, 8oz/280g, 560 yds/550m: Kettle-dyed Holly Berry, 1 skein
- Size 6 (4mm), 16"/40.5cm long circular and double-pointed needles (dpns) or size needed to obtain gauge
- Stitch markers (one in CC for beg of rnd)

Gauge
20 sts and 28 rows = 4"/10cm in St st.
Adjust needle size as necessary to obtain correct gauge.

The colorful stained-glass window on the stairway landing at the American Swedish Institute is known as the Visby Window. The man in the center panel wears a beautiful long red stocking hat. Draped over his hand is the end of another wonderfully long red stocking hat, which offered the inspiration for this pattern. The hat appears to have some texture, but it was difficult to determine the exact pattern. We used a beautiful kettle-dyed red yarn that adds a more vintage feel to the hat and is reminiscent of the oil painting depicted in the Visby Window.

Special Abbreviation
S2KP2: Slip 2 sts tog, knitwise, k1, pass the slipped sts over (this is a centered double decrease).

Instructions

With MC and circular needle, CO 100 sts. Pm for beg of rnd and join, taking care not to twist sts.

Ribbing: Work around in k2, p2 rib for 2"/5cm.

Rnds 1–53: Foll chart.

DECREASES

Place second marker after the 48th st.

Rnd 1: K1, p2, k2tog, k to 2 sts before marker, ssk, slm (slip marker), p2, k1, p2, k2tog, k to 2 sts before next marker, ssk (4 sts dec'd).

Rnds 2–12: Work in est pat.

Rep Dec Rnds 1–12 until 16 sts rem, ending after Rnd 12.

Last Dec Rnd: K1, p2, S2KP2, p2, k1, p2, S2KP2, p2—12 sts rem.

Work 11 more rnds as est, break yarn, leaving a 6"/15cm tail.

With tapestry needle, thread tail through rem sts, pull tight to close. Secure on WS.

FINISHING

Weave in all ends. Block.

The colorful stained-glass window on the stairway landing at the American Swedish Institute is known as the Visby Window. The man in the center panel wears a beautiful long red stocking hat which offered the inspiration for this pattern. The hat appears to have some texture, but it was difficult to determine the exact pattern.

Long Stocking Hat Chart

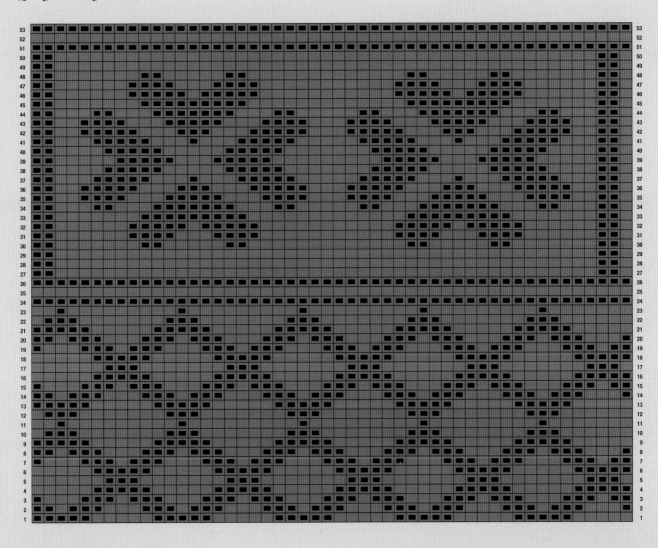

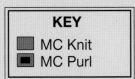

KEY
MC Knit
MC Purl

Sami Handwork: Source of Pride through Good Times and Bad

By Harley Refsal

Although the origin of the Sami people—formerly referred to as Lapps, or Laplanders—is not known with certainty, they are the indigenous people of far northern Norway, Sweden, Finland, and the Kola Peninsula in Russia. The Sami have likely inhabited these areas for thousands of years, despite the harshness of the climate.

Although many Samis once worked as fishermen, hunters, and small-scale farmers, many led lives that revolved around that magnificent and hardy animal of the Arctic North, the reindeer. Reindeer provided most of the resources the Sami people needed to survive: hides for clothing and shelter; bones and antlers for tools and weapons; and reindeer meat and milk for food. Reindeer also served as pack animals. Multigenerational groups of Sami followed the herds of reindeer as they migrated, century after century, along the same well-worn paths, up into the high mountain country during calving season, then down into the more sheltered forest regions during the coldest months of winter. Throughout their nomadic lives, the Sami never lost touch with their handwork traditions. Men crafted knives, utensils, and household items from horn and antlers; women tanned reindeer hides and made clothing, using both the hides and woven fabric. Not surprisingly, their designs were often based on elements and colors that reflected their natural surroundings. Despite the numerous physical, political, or economic hardships the Sami have experienced through the centuries, their handwork traditions remain strong and vital—a rallying point and source of cultural and artistic pride.

Sami, or Lapp, children in Lyngseidet, Norway. A few Lapp families come to Norway from Sweden every summer with herds of three to four thousand reindeer for pasture privileges.
AMERICAN SWEDISH INSTITUTE COLLECTION

Sami Hat, Scarf, and Gauntlet Mittens

The Sami people, formerly known as Lapps, are indigenous to four countries: Norway, Finland, Russia, and Sweden. The Sami keep herds of reindeer for food, much as the Native Americans relied on buffalo. We can imagine this hat being worn by the Sami people on one of their extremely cold and snowy days. The colors would brighten up even the darkest morning.

Sami Hat

Size
Adult's Average

Materials

- Cascade 220, 100% wool, 100g/3.5oz, 220yds/201m:
- 1 skein in each of the following colors:
- Blue #9457 (MC), Cream #8010 (A), Yellow #7828 (B), Green #9490 (C), Red #8895 (D)
- Size 7 (4.5mm), 16"/40.5cm long needle
- Size 8 (5mm), 16"/40.5cm long needle or size needed to obtain gauge
- Cotton waste yarn
- Stitch marker
- Tapestry needle
- Pom-pom maker (optional)

Gauge
20 sts and 24 rnds = 4"/10cm in solid color St st on larger needle.
Adjust needle size as necessary to obtain correct gauge.

Special Techniques

Crochet Cast-On (see Special Techniques Used, page 140)
Kitchener Stitch (see Special Techniques Used, page 140)

Instructions

FACING

Using Crochet Cast-On method and smaller needle, CO 96 sts. Pm for beg of rnd and join, taking care not to twist sts.
With MC, work around in St st for 5"/12.5cm.
Next Rnd (turning ridge): Purl.

MAIN HAT

Change to larger needle.
Foll Chart Rows 1–33, working around in St st.
Remove provisional CO and place live sts on smaller needle. Fold facing inside hat so that WS's are tog. *Holding the two needles parallel and using MC, knit the 1st st on the front needle and the 1st st on the back needle tog as 1 st; rep from * around until all sts of the facing are joined to the hat. At the end of this row, all the sts should be on the larger needle. With MC, work around in St st for 4"/10cm.
Using Kitchener stitch, close top of hat.

FINISHING

Weave in all ends. Block.

POM-POMS (MAKE 2)

Use pom-pom maker or follow instructions as follows:
Cut two cardboard circles the size of desired pom-pom. Cut a hole in the center of each circle, approx ½"/1.25cm in diameter. Thread a tapestry needle with one very long strand of MC, B, and D. Holding both circles together, insert needle through center hole, over the outside edge, and through center again, going around and around until entire circle is covered and center hole is filled (thread more lengths of yarn as needed). With sharp scissors, cut yarn between the two circles all around the circumference. Using two 12"/30.5cm strands of yarn (tying ends), wrap yarn between circles, going two or three times around; pull tight and tie into a firm knot. Remove cardboard and fluff out the pom-pom. Trim ends as necessary to make pom-pom circular. Attach a pom-pom to each point on top of hat.

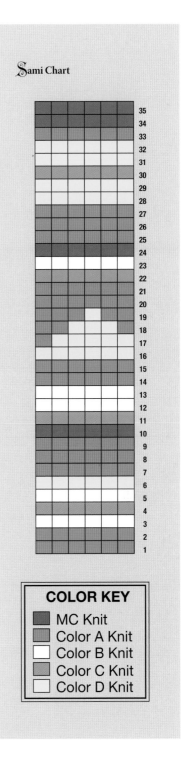

Sami Chart

COLOR KEY
- MC Knit
- Color A Knit
- Color B Knit
- Color C Knit
- Color D Knit

Sami Scarf

Finished Measurements

9"/23cm wide x 66"/167.5cm
long

Materials

- Cascade 220, 100% wool,
  100g/3.5oz, 220yds/201m:
- Blue #9457 (MC), 4 skeins
- Cream #8010 (A), Yellow
  #7828 (B), Green #9490 (C),
  Red #8895 (D), 1 skein each
- Size 8 (5mm), 16"/40.5cm
  long circular needles or size
  needed to obtain gauge (2)
- Crochet hook size I-9
  (5mm)
- Cotton waste yarn
- Tapestry needle
- Stitch markers (2)

Gauge

20 sts and 24 rnds = 4"/10cm
in solid color St st on larger
needle.
*Adjust needle size as neces-
sary to obtain correct gauge.*

The Sami people live in a part of Scandinavia where for long periods of time, the sun doesn't set. But don't let the sun fool you: it's still mighty cold! This scarf is great for bundling up on those bitter cold winter days. The color pattern is repeated on both ends, and for warmth, the scarf is knit double. This scarf is the perfect accessory to the Sami Hat. Knit this one for yourself or to give to a loved one.

Special Techniques
Provisional Cast-On (see Special Techniques Used, page 140)

Instructions

SCARF FIRST HALF

With waste yarn, and using the provisional method, CO 84 sts. Place first marker for beg of rnd and second marker after 42 sts to mark the center. Join, taking care not to twist sts.

Foll chart, working 33 rnds of colorwork.

Change to MC and work around in St st until for 27"/68.5cm above last row of colorwork (center of scarf).

Turn piece inside out and weave in ends. Unravel provisional cast-on and, using Kitchener stitch, close the beg end tog.

Faux side seam: Remove first marker at beg of rnd. Drop the 1st st all the way down to the colorwork section and stop before it unravels into the colorwork. With crochet hook, slip st back up the "bars" created by dropping the st two at a time (if this were a dropped st you would pick up one "bar" at a time; however, to make this seam pronounced, you will be picking up two "bars" at a time, which will make the scarf lie flat create a decorative effect).

Rep the dropped st in the same manner after the second marker. Keep sts on needle.

SCARF SECOND HALF

Rep for second half using second needle and keeping the second half on your needle.

FINISHING

Using Kitchener stitch, join the two halves tog.
Weave in all ends. Block.

OLD SWEDISH RECIPE

SWEDISH PANCAKES/ PANNKAKKOR

Delicious Swedish pancakes can be made ahead of time, cooled, and served with lingonberry jam and whipped cream for a traditional dessert. This recipe was provided by my daughter's Nordic ski teammate Malin Eriksson, an exchange student from Sweden.

4 eggs
2 c. milk
½ c. flour
1 tbsp. sugar
1 pinch salt
2 tbsp. butter, melted

In a large bowl, beat eggs with a wire whisk. Mix in milk, flour, sugar, salt, and melted butter. Preheat a nonstick skillet to medium heat. Pour a thin layer of batter on skillet, spreading to edges. Cook until top surface appears dry, then flip with a spatula. Cook until golden brown. For dessert, spread with lingonberry jam and top with whipped cream.

Set of wool felt Sami hats.
AMERICAN SWEDISH
INSTITUTE COLLECTION

Size
Adult's Average

Finished Measurements
Circumference at palm:
8"/20.5cm
Length: 14"/35cm

Materials

- Cascade 220, 100% wool, 100g/3.5oz, 220yds/201m:
- Blue #9457 (MC), 2 skeins
- 1 skein in each of the following colors:
- Cream #8010 (A), Yellow #7828 (B), Green #9490 (C), Red #8895 (D)
- Cascade Eco Duo, 70% undyed baby alpaca/30% undyed Merino wool, 100g/3.5oz, 197yds/180m: Tan and Cream #1702 (E), 1 skein
- Set size 8 (5mm) double-pointed needles or size needed to obtain gauge
- Set size 6 (4mm) double-pointed needles or two sizes smaller than size needed to obtain gauge
- Size 7 (4.5mm), 16"/40.5cm long circular needle
- Cotton waste yarn
- Stitch markers (2)
- Tapestry needle

Gauge
20 sts and 24 rnds = 4"/10cm in solid color St st on larger needle.
Adjust needle size as necessary to obtain correct gauge.

Sami Gauntlet Mittens

Special Techniques
Provisional Cast-On (see Special Techniques Used, page 140)

Mitten Instructions (Make 2)

FACING

Using waste yarn and provisional cast-on method, CO 48 sts. Pm for beg of rnd and join, taking care not to twist sts. Change to MC and divide sts evenly on larger dpns.

Rnd 1: Knit.
Rnd 2: Knit, inc 6 sts evenly spaced on rnd—54 sts.

Rnds 3–34: Knit.

Rnd 35: Purl for turning ridge.

GAUNTLET

Rnds 36–67: Foll Chart Rows 1–32.

Rnd 68: Work Row 33 of chart, working k2tog evenly spaced across rnd six times—48 sts.

Rnds 69–71: Work last 3 rows of chart.

Remove provisional CO and place live sts on smaller needle. Fold facing inside of mitten so that WS's are tog. *Holding the two needles parallel and using MC, knit the 1st st on the front needle and the 1st st on the back needle tog as 1 st; rep from * around until all sts of the facing are joined to the gauntlet. At the end of this row, all the sts should be on the larger needle.

Change to smaller dpns and dec 8 sts evenly around—40 sts.

RIBBING

With MC, work in k1, p1 rib for 6 rnds.

Change to larger dpns.

MAIN MITTEN

Rnd 1: Knit, inc 2 sts evenly spaced around—42 sts.

Rnds 2–4: Knit.

THUMB GUSSET

Rnd 5: K20, pm, k1f&b, k1f&b, pm, k20—44 sts.

Rnd 6: Knit.

Rnd 7: K to marker, k1f&b, k to 1 st before marker, k1f&b, k to end of rnd.

Rep last 2 rnds until there are 16 sts between markers.

HAND

Next Rnd: Knit to marker, remove marker, k1, place next 14 sts on holder, k1, remove marker, k to end of rnd—42 sts.

Cont even until mitten length is even with height of pinky finger.

TOP OF MITTEN

Rnd 1: (K4, k2tog) seven times around—35 sts.

Rnd 2: Knit.

Rnd 3: (K3, k2tog) seven times around—28 sts.

Rnd 4: Knit.

Rnd 5: (K2, k2tog) seven times around—21 sts.

Rnd 6: Knit.

Rnd 7: (K1, k2tog) seven times around—14 sts.

Rnd 8: Knit.

Rnd 9: (K2tog) seven times—7 sts.

Break yarn, leaving a 6"/15cm tail. Using tapestry needle, thread tail through rem sts, pull tight, and weave in end.

OLD SWEDISH RECIPE

SWEDISH PEA SOUP

Yellow pea soup and Swedish pancakes are traditionally served on Thursday nights in Sweden.

1 lb. dried split yellow peas (Swedish soup uses yellow, not green peas)

8 c. water

2 c. onions, finely chopped

1 peeled whole onion, studded with cloves (optional)

1 large carrot, chopped (about ½ c)

1 meaty ham bone or 2–3 ham hocks

1 tsp. dried thyme

1 tsp. ground ginger

1 tsp. salt

⅛ tsp. pepper

Rinse peas. Fill a large soup pot with 8 cups of water. Add peas, chopped onions, whole onion with cloves, chopped carrots, and ham bone. Bring to a boil, then cover and reduce to a simmer for 90 minutes. Remove 2–3 cups, puree in a blender, and return to the pot. Simmer another 30–60 minutes. Thirty minutes before serving, remove the whole onion with cloves and the meat. Chop the meat and return to the pot. Season the soup with thyme, ginger, salt, and pepper. Simmer for 15 minutes more. Serve and enjoy on a Thursday night, Swedish style.

THUMB

Distributing sts evenly on 3 dpns, sl 14 thumb gusset sts to larger dpns; then, with MC, pick up and k2 sts at thumb opening, pm for beg of rnd—16 sts.

Work even in St st until thumb is 2 ¾"/7cm or until thumb height is even with thumb nail height.

Dec Rnd: (K2, k2tog) four times—12 sts.

Work 2 rnds even.

Dec Rnd: (K1, ktog) four times—8 sts.

Work 1 rnd even.

Dec Rnd: (K2tog) four times—4 sts.

Break yarn, leaving a 6"/15cm tail. Using tapestry needle, thread tail through rem sts, pull tight, and weave in end.

MITTEN LINING

Turn mitten inside out. Using E, beg at the base of the mitten ribbing, pick up and k40 sts around.

Work lining as for mitten from ribbing directions to thumb directions. Turn mittens right side out, making sure mitten lining lies smoothly inside mitten.

Jmmigrant Hood

Size
Woman's Average

Finished Measurements
Head width: 16"/40.5 cm
Length: 18"/45.5cm

Materials

- Cascade 220, 100% wool, 100g/3.75oz, 220yds/201m: Ireland Green Hunter #2429, 2 skeins
- Size 7 (4.5mm), 16"/40.5cm long circular needle or size needed to obtain gauge
- Spare needle of the same size or smaller
- Waste yarn
- Stitch markers (2)
- Safety pins (2)

Gauge
16 sts and 20 rows = 4"/10cm in pat.
Adjust needle size as necessary to obtain correct gauge.

One item in the ASI's Swedish Life Exhibit that caught our eye was this shaggy immigrant hood. It was worn by the donor's grandmother, Elsa Trulson, when she immigrated to America from Skäne, Sweden, in 1872. The original bonnet was made with netting and was lined with plain knit. This updated version is knit in a stitch that looks like crochet, but is really a clever use of multiple "triple wraps" to create an openwork stitch.

Special Techniques
Crochet Cast-On (see Special Techniques Used, page 140)
Kitchener Stitch (see Special Techniques Used, page 140)

The Immigrant Hood was inspired by this wool bonnet with shoulder cape, worn by the donor's grandmother, Elsa Trulson, when she immigrated to America from Skäne, Sweden, in 1872. Donated by Elenor Lloyd.

AMERICAN SWEDISH INSTITUTE COLLECTION

Pattern Notes

The hood is made first and then the capelet is added by picking up stitches along the neckline selvage. Increases are worked between the pattern repeats to create the shaping necessary for a well-fitting hood and cape.

Instructions

With MC and waste yarn, using the crochet cast-on method, CO 80 sts.

Rows 1, 3, and 5: Purl.

Rows 2 and 4: Knit

Row 6: Unzip sts held on waste yarn and place on second needle; fold work in half with the purl side showing. Hold working side in front, waste yarn sts in back, and needles parallel. *Insert right needle tip into first st on front needle, then into the first st on back needle and knit them tog; rep from * around—80 sts.

Pattern Stitch

Row 1: K1, *insert needle into st as if to k, wind yarn around three times, k st; rep from * until 1 st from end, k1.

Row 2: K1, *(remove loops from needle and place long sts onto right needle) three times, transfer 3 long sts back to left needle, and (k, p, k) into all 3 sts at once; rep from * until 1 st from end, k1.

Row 3: Knit.

Row 4: Knit.

Row 5: Rep Row 1.

Row 6: Rep Row 2.

Row 7: Knit.

Row 8: Place marker after 31st and 49th sts. K to first marker, (k1, k 1f&b) nine times, k to end slipping second marker—89 sts.

Rows 9–31: Rep Rows 1–4 six times, ending before last knit row of rep.

Row 32: K to first marker, (k2, k2tog) six times, k to end slipping second marker—83 sts.

Rows 33–35: Rep Rows 1–3.

Row 36: K to marker, k1, (k1, k2tog) six times, k to end slipping second marker—77 sts.

Rows 37–39: Rep Rows 1–3.

Row 40: K to marker, k2, (k2tog) six times, k to end slipping second marker—71 sts.

Rows 41–43: Rep Rows 1–3.

Row 44: K34, k2tog; break yarn at this point, leaving a long tail. Fold work in half and weave together using Kitchener st.

CAPE

Along selvage edge, pick up and k92 sts.

Row 1: K1, *insert needle into st as if to k, wind yarn around three times, k st; rep from * until 1 st from end, k1.

Row 2: K1, (remove loops from needle and place long sts onto right needle) three times, transfer 3 long sts back to left needle, and (k, p, k) into all 3 sts at once; rep until 1 st from end, k1.

Row 3: Knit.

Row 4: Knit.

Rows 5–7: Rep Rows 1–3.

Row 8: K1, (k1, k1f&b, k1) thirty times, k1—122 sts.

Rows 9–11: Rep Rows 1–3.

Row 12: K1, (k2, k1f&b, k1) thirty times, k1—152 sts.

Rows 13–15: Rep Rows 1–3.

Row 16: K1, (k2, k1f&b, k2) thirty times, k1—182 sts.

Rows 17–19: Rep Rows 1–3.

Row 20: K1, (k3, k1f&b, k2) thirty times, k1—212 sts.

Rows 21–23: Rep Rows 1–3.

Row 24: K1, (k3, k1f&b, k3) thirty times, k1—242 sts.

Rows 25–27: Rep Rows 1–3.

Row 28: K1, (k4, k1f&b, k3) thirty times, k1—272 sts.

Rows 29–31: Rep Rows 1–3.

Row 32: Knit.

Row 33: BO in purl st.

FINISHING

Weave in all ends. Block.

Use the same pattern stitch from the Immigrant Hood pattern to make the ethereal Immigrant Mist Cowl.

Immigrant Mist Cowl

Using light and airy mohair with the same beautiful pattern stitch as in the Immigrant Hood, this cowl is reminiscent of the harbor mist many immigrants saw when they first arrived in the New World.

Instructions

CO 136 sts. Pm for beg of rnd and join, taking care not to twist sts.

Rnds 1–2: Knit.

PATTERN STITCH

Rnd 3: *Insert needle into st as if to k, wind yarn around three times, k st; rep from * around.

Rnd 4: (Remove loops from needle and place long sts onto right needle) three times, transfer 3 long sts back to left needle, and (k, p, k) into all 3 sts at once; rep from * around.

Rnd 5: Knit.

Rnd 6: Knit.

Rep Rnds 3–6 until there are 14 reps of pat.

BO loosely.

FINISHING

Weave in all ends.

Size

Woman's Average

Finished Measurements

Circumference: 28"/71cm

Height: 16"/40.5cm

Materials

LACE

- Rowan Kid Silk Haze, 70% super kid mohair/30% silk, 25g/.875g, 229yds/209m: Pearl #590, 1 skein
- Size 10 (6mm), 16"/40.5cm long circular needle or size needed to obtain gauge
- Stitch marker

Gauge

20 sts = 4"/10cm pat.

Adjust needle size as necessary to obtain correct gauge.

CHAPTER 2

Clever Knitting with Embellishments

A blue Dala horse statute near the cemetery at Gammelgården Museum, Scandia, Minnesota.

The embellishments and techniques used in each of these projects are great additions to otherwise basic knitting. Check out the woven look on the Dala Horse sweater—it's simple, yet makes a remarkable statement and pays homage to one of the Swedes' other very distinct textiles traditions: weaving.

Glass Bag

Finished Measurements
Before felting: 38"/91.5cm high and 45"/114.5cm around
After felting: 24"/61cm high and 34"/86.5cm around

Materials

4 MEDIUM

- Cascade 220, 100% wool, 100g/3.5oz, 220yds/208m:
- Black #8555 (A), 5 skeins
- Noro Kureyon, 100% wool, 50g/1.75oz, 109yds/100m:
- Color #170 (B), 2 skeins
- Size 10 ½ (6.5mm), 29"/73.5cm long circular needle or size needed to obtain gauge
- Size 10 ½ (6.5mm) double-pointed needles or size needed to obtain gauge
- Stitch markers (9)
- Tapestry needle
- Clover needle felting tool #8900 and needle felting needles 36 gauge #8906
- Clover felting mat, size large #8911
- Tear-away stabilizer, lightweight

Gauge
24 sts and 26 rows = 4"/10cm before felting.
Adjust needle as necessary to obtain correct gauge.

Sweden is well known for its glasswork, and the American Swedish Institute has an extensive collection. The cutout design on this bag was inspired by a hand-blown glass piece designed by Andrea Blum and Warren Olson using the Swedish *graal* technique. Both are passionate glass designers and collectors from Minneapolis. We used Noro Kureyon to create the color insert in the bag. The repeats in the yarn worked beautifully. Use the color we did, one of your choosing, or even two different colors and you too will feel the flow of the glass in the movement of the colors!

Folk Art Tulips, by Andrea Blum and Warren Olson, inspired the cutout design on the Glass Bag. To make the vase, Blum and Olson used a background Ariel technique. A Nordic sidesaddle cover dating to the nineteenth century inspired the design on the vase.

AMERICAN SWEDISH INSTITUTE COLLECTION, PHOTOGRAPH BY SUE FLANDERS

Instructions

COLOR INSERT

Using B and circular needle, CO 40 sts. *Do not join.*
Row 1: Knit.
Row 2: Purl.
Row 3: Change to A and knit.
Row 4: Purl.
Row 5: Change back to B and knit.
Rep Rows 2–5 until you have used almost all of the two skeins.
BO. Weave in ends.

BAG BODY

Using A and circular needle, CO 180 sts. Pm for beg of rnd and join, being careful not to twist sts.
Rnd 1: Knit.
Rnd 2: Purl.
Rep Rnds 1 and 2 three more times.
Cont knitting every rnd for 38"/96.5cm.
Rep Rnds 1 and 2 two times. On last rnd, place a marker every 20 sts for a total of nine markers.

DECREASE FOR BOTTOM OF BAG

Rnd 1: (K18, k2tog) nine times.
Rnd 2: Knit.
Rep Rnds 1 and 2 until 9 sts rem, having 1 st less between decs every other rnd and changing to dpns when necessary.
Cut tail leaving a 6"/15cm tail. Thread tail thru rem 9 sts on dpns. Weave in ends.

HANDLE

Using A and 2 dpns, CO 20 sts.
Row 1: K to last 3 sts, yf, sl as if to p last 3 sts.
Rep Row 1 for 45"/114.5cm.
BO. Weave in ends.

FINISHING

Full the bag, handle, and color insert in washing machine until they reach finished measurements or desired size. Let dry.
Trace shapes onto tear-away stabilizer paper in position as shown. Using leftover Cascade 220 in black, sew the stabilizer paper onto bag. Cut out the shapes.
Brush back of Glass Bag with needle felting mat before needle felting the color insert to the bag. Using needle felting tool and mat, needle felt color insert to bag.
Trim handle to desired shape and length. Using machine, sew handles into place on sides.
Make twisted cord (see page 141).
Weave cords through bag to make drawstring closure.

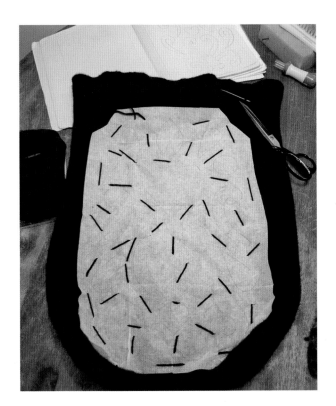

Glass Bag Template

Stained-Glass Hat

Size
Adult's Medium/Large

Finished Measurements
Circumference at head:
20"/51cm
Height: 10"/25.5cm

Materials

- Noro Kureyon, 100% wool, 50g/1.75oz, 108yd/99m:
- Color #170, 2 skeins
- Size 8 (5mm), 16"/40,5cm long circular and double-pointed needles or size needed to obtain gauge
- Stitch markers (5)
- Tapestry needle

Gauge
18 sts and 10 rows = 4"/10cm in Garter st.
20 sts and 28 rows = 4"/10cm) in St st.
Adjust needle size as necessary to obtain correct gauge.

The Swedish are known for their beautiful handmade glass. The ASI's glass collection pays homage to this rich tradition by showcasing exquisite glass pieces that draw you in and beg to be looked at up close. Many of these pieces served as inspiration for the patterns in this book, including the Stained-Glass Hat. The color progression in Noro Kureyon makes knitting this hat an adventure. When we knit this hat, we could hardly wait to get to the next section of color to see how it would spill out of the skein. The color combinations reminded us of how melted glass blends together into mesmerizing fields of wonder. The hat is constructed employing a traditional modular knitting technique called Domino knitting. The squares that make up this hat show off the self-striping yarn perfectly.

Special Techniques

Bind-Off in I-cord: Using needles two to three sizes larger than main needles, CO 3 extra sts at beg of BO row, *k next 2 sts and sl the 3rd st knitwise, then k 1 more st (4 sts on right needle). Pass the slipped st over the last knitted st (3 sts on right needle). Sl these 3 sts back onto left needle purlwise. Tug on working yarn to tighten up sts. Rep from * until only 3 sts remain. Cut yarn and draw through remaining sts.

Special Abbreviations

A = Head circumference (20"/51cm or desired size)
B = Earlobe (10"/25.5cm height over head to earlobe or desired height)

Project Notes

To customize hat, make strip of squares shorter than you desire, as Garter stitch is stretchy.

If hat is "deep" and will measure more than measurement B, then customize hat by skipping or working fewer hem edge Garter stitch ridges. For flat top of hat, skip the plain knit row between decrease rows.

Block hat on a balloon blown to measurement A.

Use needles two to three sizes larger than main needles in your right hand to do I-cord BO.

If using multiple yarns, remember to change colors whenever you like.

Try using different textures as well as colors

Instructions

DOMINO SECTION

First Strip

Square 1: CO 20 sts.
Row 1 and all odd rows (WS): K to last st, sl 1 wyif.
Row 2 (RS): K8, K2tog, ssk, k8.
Row 4: K7, k2tog, ssk, k7.
Row 6: K6, k2tog, ssk, k6.
Row 8: K5, k2tog, ssk, k5.
Row 10: K4, k2tog, ssk, k4.
Row 12: K3, k2tog, ssk, k3.
Row 14: K2, k2tog, ssk, k2.
Row 16: K1, k2tog, ssk, k1.
Row 18: K2tog, ssk.
Row 20: K2tog.
Note: Only cut yarn if you are changing yarn; no need to cut if using a self-striping yarn.

Square 2: Pick up and k10 sts along side edge; CO 10 sts—20 sts.
Work Rows 1–20 of Square 1.
Rep Square 2 until strip measure 1"–2"/2.5–5cm less than measurement A, depending on desired fit. **Note**: This would be between seven and nine squares (sample is nine squares).

OLD SWEDISH RECIPE
SWEDISH ROLLS

This traditional cinnamon Swedish roll is not sweet like its American counterpart, the cinnamon roll. It is made with baking powder instead of yeast, so it is quicker to prepare. These rolls were prepared and served by the nuns in the cafeteria at the College of St. Benedict in St. Joseph, Minnesota, where Sue went to college.

3 ½ c. + 1 tbsp flour
1 tsp. baking powder
1 tsp. baking soda
1 tsp. salt
½ c. + 2 tbsp. sugar
½ c. shortening
2 eggs
½ c. + 2 ½ tbsp. buttermilk
½ c. butter, softened
1 c. brown sugar

Combine dry ingredients in a large mixing bowl. Cut in shortening until mixture resembles course meal. In a separate bowl, combine eggs and buttermilk. Add eggs and buttermilk to flour mixture, mixing just until moist; do not overmix. Divide dough into two parts. Roll each piece into ½-inch-thick circle. Brush dough with soft butter, sprinkle with brown sugar, roll up, and slice into rolls ½-inch thick.

Bake at 350°F for 20 minutes or until golden brown on the edges.

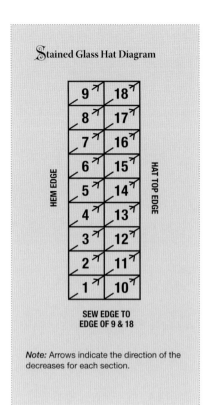

Stained Glass Hat Diagram

SEW EDGE TO
EDGE OF 9 & 18

Note: Arrows indicate the direction of the decreases for each section.

Second Strip
Square 1: CO 10 sts; pick up and k10 sts along side of Square 1 of First Strip—20 sts.
Work Rows 1–20 of Square 1.

Square 2: Pick up and k10 sts along Square 1 of Second Strip and 10 sts along edge of First Strip—20 sts.
Work Rows 1–20 of Square 1.
Rep Square 2 of Second Strip to match length of First Strip.
Sew strips together. Weave in ends.

HAT TOP
With circular needle, pick up and k10 sts for every square made.
Example: Ten squares would equal 100 sts picked up (making sure the number picked up is a multiple of five).
Work 3 Garter st ridges. **Note**: Garter st in the rnd is k 1 rnd, p 1 rnd.
K 1 rnd; at the same time, starting at the beginning of the rnd, place 5 markers evenly around.
Rnd 1: *K to 2 sts before marker; k2tog; rep from * around.
Rnd 2: K 1 rnd.
Rep Rnds 1 and 2 until 5 sts remain, removing markers on last row and changing to dpns as needed.
Break yarn, leaving a 2-yard tail, and work tail through rem sts.

TOP KNOT
Using dpns and tail used for Hat Top, pick up and k4 sts.
Work I-cord for 2–2.5"/5–6.5cm. BO.
Weave in ends. Tie knot like a balloon.

HAT HEM
Pick up and knit the same number of sts as you did for Hat Top.
Work 3 Garter st ridges. BO in I-cord.
Weave in ends.

Circle of Hearts Bag

Finished Measurements (After Fulling)

Width: 16"/40.5cm
Length: 12"/30.5cm

Materials

- Cascade 220, 100% wool, 100g/3.5oz, 220yds/201m:
- Cream #8505, 4 skeins
- Size 9 (5.5mm), 16"/40.5cm long circular needle
- Stitch markers
- Tapestry needle

Embellishment Materials

- Cascade 220, 100% wool, 100g/3.5oz, 220yds/201m
- 1 skein each of the following:
- Forrest #9429 (A), Brick Red #9413 (B), Royal Blue #7817 (C), Old Gold #7826 (D)
- 3"/7.5cm heart- or mitten-shaped cookie cutter for tracing cutouts
- Sharp embroidery needle and thimble
- Tapestry yarn to match contracting colors selected
- One pair 24"/61cm sewn round, solid leather core handles ("sew on" style from Homestead Heirlooms; kit also contains coordinating waxed linen and wooden anchor buttons).

Gauge

15 sts and 20 rnds = 4"/10cm in St st with single strand of yarn.
Gauge is not essential for this project; just make sure your stitches are loose and airy.

The motif of four hearts positioned in a circle appears frequently in Scandinavian textiles. It is most commonly seen on the small bags worn for decoration with traditional costumes. An accessory bag, part of a child's costume displayed in the ASI regional exhibit, inspired this design. Mrs. Clarence Bros donated the original child's costume in 1982. The colors in the apron are repeated in the bag's decorative embroidery.

The Circle of Hearts Bag was designed to be more functional than the original costume pouch. This bag features a larger compartment and leather handles for carrying. The circle of four hearts can also be made with a circle of four mittens, if desired. The bag and the contrasting colored pieces of knitting are knit and then fulled. The designs are then traced and cut out of the fulled piece and embroidered onto the bag.

Dalarna girl's costume purse from Rättvik parish. The skirt in the background shows the distinctive horizontal stripes, which are characteristic of the Rättvik costume. Donated by Misses Margaret and Matilida Wallblom in 1965.

AMERICAN SWEDISH
INSTITUTE COLLECTION

Special Techniques

Fulling (see Special Techniques Used, page 140).
Kitchener Stitch (see Special Techniques Used, page 140)

Pattern Notes

Embroidery is done after fulling to finished size.

Instructions

With two strands of MC, CO 136 sts. Pm for beg of rnd and after 68th st and join, taking care not to twist sts.
Work in St st for 24"/61cm.

DECREASES

Rnd 1: K1, ssk, k to within 3 sts of marker, k2tog, k2, ssk, k to 3 sts from end, k2tog, k1.
Rnd 2: Knit.
Rep dec rnd every other rnd three more times—120 sts.
Break yarn, leaving a long tail.
With tapestry needle and using Kitchener stitch, close the bottom of bag.

FINISHING

Full bag in the washing machine (it may take more than one cycle to get the proper shrinkage).

The two sides of the Circle of Hearts Bag.

MOTIFS

Note: With contracting colors, knit a swatch from which the motifs will be cut. It is easiest to knit in the round and cut open later.
With 16"/40.5cm circular needle, CO 70 sts. Pm for beg of rnd and join, taking care not to twist sts. Work in St st for 6"/16cm. Change to the next color and cont until 6"/15cm of all four colors are knit on the swatch. Full the swatch in the washing machine to shrink. Cut this tube open and lay flat to dry.

Using the cookie cutter as a template, trace around the chosen shape, cutting out one heart or mitten from each color. On each cutout, stitch a two-color lazy daisy in the middle of each motif. The lazy daisy has eight petals: four that are north, south, east, and west (main) in one color and four additional petals in between the first ones (contrast). Make a small French knot in the center.

Cutout A: Use D for main petals and French knot, then use B for the contrast petals.
Cutout B: Use C for main petals and French knot, then use A for the contrast petals.
Cutout C: Use B for main petals and French knot, then use D for the contrast petals.
Cutout D: Use D for main petals and French knot, then use C for the contrast petals.

Lay the cutouts on the bag and position into a circle (use the close-up photo as a guide for placement). Make sure you allow enough room on the top edge for the handle attachment. Using contrasting tapestry thread, embroider blanket stitch around the shape to secure to bag.
Note: This is where the thimble may be needed to prevent injury.

Cutout A: Blanket stitch with C, and stitch four petal daisy at top in B.
Cutout B: Blanket stitch with D, and stitch four petal daisy at top in A.
Cutout C: Blanket stitch with A, and stitch four petal daisy at top in D.
Cutout D: Blanket stitch with B, and stitch four petal daisy at top in C.

Finally, stitch daisy in the middle of the circle using B for the main petals and D for the contrast petals.

Follow manufacturer's directions to attach leather handles.

OLD SWEDISH RECIPE

SWEDISH RICE DESSERT WITH CRIMSON RASPBERRY SAUCE

Makes 1 ½ cups

This recipe has been in Sue's collection for a long time. She got it after tasting the dessert at a holiday potluck. The almond-flavored rice pudding goes nicely with the raspberry sauce, and the ruby red color gives it that extra special touch for the holidays.

½ c. uncooked short-grain white rice

1 pt. whole milk

½ tsp. salt

1 envelope plain gelatin

¼ c. cold water

1 pt. whipping cream

⅓ c. sugar

½ tsp. almond extract

In a small saucepan, bring rice and milk to a boil. Reduce heat and simmer until thick and creamy, about 20–25 minutes, stirring occasionally since milk burns and boils over easily. Add salt. Dissolve gelatin in cold water and add to hot rice mixture. Let cool until it begins to set (about 20 minutes). Whip cream, add sugar and almond extract, and mix with rice. Pour into a 1 ¼ quart mold. Refrigerate until ready to serve, then invert onto a serving plate. Serve with Crimson Raspberry Sauce.

Crimson Raspberry Sauce

12 oz. whole frozen raspberries

1 ½ tsp. cornstarch

½ c. red currant jelly

Thaw and crush raspberries, then thoroughly combine with cornstarch. Add red currant jelly and bring to a boil. Cook and stir until mixture is clear and thickens slightly. Chill.

Dala Horse Sweater

Sizes
Child's 2 (4, 6) years

Finished Measurements
Chest: 22 (24, 26)"/56 (61, 66)cm
Length: 13 (14 ½, 15 ½)"/33 (37, 39.5)cm

Materials

- Cascade 220 Superwash Sport, 100% superwash Merino wool, 50g/1.75oz, 36yds/33m:
- Red #809 (MC), 3 (3, 4) skeins
- Yellow #820 (A), Mint #1942 (B), Teal #845 (C), 1 skein each
- Sizes 2 (2.75mm) and 4 (3.5mm), 16"/40.5cm long circular needles or size needed to obtain gauge
- Size 2 (2.75mm) and 4 (3.5mm) double-pointed needles
- Small size crochet hook
- Stitch markers
- Stitch holders
- Piece of cardboard the same size as sweater
- Tapestry needle

Gauge
24 sts and 32 rnds = 4"/10cm in St st using larger needles. *Adjust needle size as necessary to obtain correct gauge.*

When the ASI sponsored a special exhibit on the Dala horse in 2002, Minnesota weaver Kelly Marshall was inspired to create the geometric Dala horse weaving. Kelly's bright and cheery piece, with its three-dimensional tail and mane, were the perfect motif for a child's sweater. The weaving is made in the traditional Rep weave technique, where the warp colors show the design and the weft is the binder that doesn't show.

In the sweater, the basic horse pattern is worked in seed stitch and then afterwards a thread is worked in the purl bumps, similar to weaving, to create the stripes on the horse. Chain stitch is then worked around the horse outline and the tail and mane are tied on to complete the horse.

Special Techniques

Kitchener Stitch (see Special Techniques Used, page 140)

Special Abbreviations

S2KP2: Slip 2 sts tog knitwise, k1, pass the slipped sts over (this is centered double dec).

Pattern Notes

Instructions for the Matching Stuffed Horse are given at the end.

Instructions

With smaller circular needle and MC, CO 116 (124, 132) sts. Pm for beg of rnd and join, taking care not to twist sts.

Work around in k2, p2 rib for 1 ½ (2, 2)"/4 (5, 5)cm. Change to larger circular needle.

Next Rnd: Knit, inc 12 (16, 16) sts evenly spaced around—128 (140, 148) sts.

Knit 5 (5, 7) more rnds.

HORSE MOTIF

Rnd 1: With MC k7 (10, 12) sts, pm, foll chart across 50 sts working horse motif in seed st, pm. With MC k rem sts.

Cont as est, working horse motif in seed st and rem sts in St st until piece measures 7 ½ (8 ½, 9)"/19 (21, 23)cm from CO.

DIVIDE FOR ARMHOLES

Place the last 64 (70, 74) sts on circular needle or holder for back.

FRONT

Cont working back and forth on the rem 64 (70, 74) sts for front until horse motif is complete. Then cont working back and forth on front sts in St st until piece measures 3 (3 ½, 4)"/7.5 (9, 10)cm from armhole split. Place center 14 (18, 20) sts on holder for neck, leaving 25 (26, 27) sts on each side of neck on needle.

LEFT NECK SHAPING

Row 1: K1, ssk, k to end.
Row 2: P.
Rep Rows 1 and 2 until 20 sts rem.
Cont even in St st until armhole measures 5 ½ (6, 6 ½)"/14 (15, 16.5)cm. Place rem sts on holder.

RIGHT NECK SHAPING

Row 1: K to within 3 sts from end, k2tog, k1.
Row 2: Purl.
Rep Rows 1 and 2 until 20 sts rem.
Cont even in St st until armhole measures 5 ½ (6, 6 ½)"/15 (15, 16.5)cm. Place rem sts on holder.

BACK

Place 64 (70, 74) back sts from holder onto needle. Work back and forth

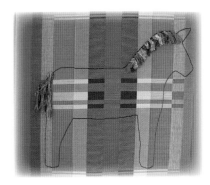

Dala horse weaving by Minnesota weaver Kelly Marshall, 2002.
AMERICAN SWEDISH INSTITUTE
COLLECTION

PHOTO BY SIDNEY GERHARDT

in St st until armhole measures 5 (5 ½, 6)"/12.5 (14, 15)cm. Place center 20 (26, 30) sts on holder for neck, leaving 22 sts on each side of neck on needle.

Rep neck shaping for left and right side as for fronts until 20 sts rem. Leave sts on needle. Place front sts on spare needle and work Kitchener stitch or three-needle bind-off to join shoulders.

SLEEVES

Note: The sleeves are worked in a seed st and stripe pat. The first rnd of the new color is knit; the next 7 rnds are worked in seed st as est.

With RS facing, using A and larger dpns, pick up and k60 (66, 72) sts around armhole.

Pm in first st (this will be the center underarm st) and join.

Rnd 1: *K1, p1; rep from * to end of rnd.

Rnd 2: Work in seed st, having a p st over a k st and a k st over a p st and ending 1 st before end of rnd.

Rnd 3: S2KP2, work rem sts in est seed st.

Rnds 4–6: Rep Rnds 1–3 once.

Rnd 7: Work in seed st.

Change to B.

Rnd 1: Knit.

Rnds 2–7: Rep Rnds 1–3 of A stripe twice.

Rnd 8: Work in seed st.

Change to C.

Rnd 1: Knit.

Rnds 2–7: Rep Rnds 1–3 of A stripe twice.

Rnd 8: Work in seed st.

Cont to work the stripe/seed pat, alternating colors A, B, and C every eight rows and at the same time, working the centered dec every 3rd rnd until 40 (48, 52) sts rem. Work in est stripe sequence until sleeve measures 6 (8, 9)"/15 (20.5, 23) cm from beg.

Change to MC, and smaller dpns.

Next Rnd: K, dec to 36 (44, 48) sts. Work around in k2, p2, ribbing for 1 ½ (2, 2)"/4 (5, 5)cm. BO in ribbing.

FINISHING

Block sweater to desired dimensions.

Dala Horse "Weaving"

Cut a piece of cardboard to match the sweater size. Slide cardboard inside body of the sweater. Starting at the left side of horse and leaving a long tail for the chain st detail, use a blunt tapestry needle to weave the yarn under each purl bump along the length of the horse pat (shown in photo). Weave five columns of each color inside the horse pat. Work chain sts around the outside edges of horse.

Fringe Detail

Using one length of each pastel color, fold yarn over crochet hook and pull loop through chain sts; place ends through folded end and pull to secure. Place fringe along the back of neck for mane.

DALA HORSE SWEATER DIAGRAM

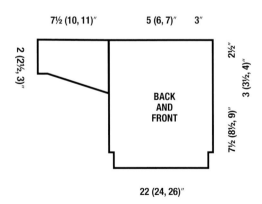

7½ (10, 11)"   5 (6, 7)"   3"

2 (2½, 3)"

2½"

3 (3½, 4)"

BACK AND FRONT

7½ (8½, 9)"

22 (24, 26)"

Tail

Cut twelve lengths, four of each pastel color. Fold yarns over crochet hook and pull loop through chain sts at tail of horse; place ends through folded end and pull to secure. If there is a concern about the tail being pulled off by child, it can be secured by sewing on the inside.

MATCHING STUFFED HORSE

Follow the Dala Horse Garland horse pat but double the MC and use size 8 (5mm) double-pointed needles to make this larger horse. Omit the Lazy Daisy and Zigzag stitch embroidered on the horse. Sew mane and tail in similar fashion as on the sweater.

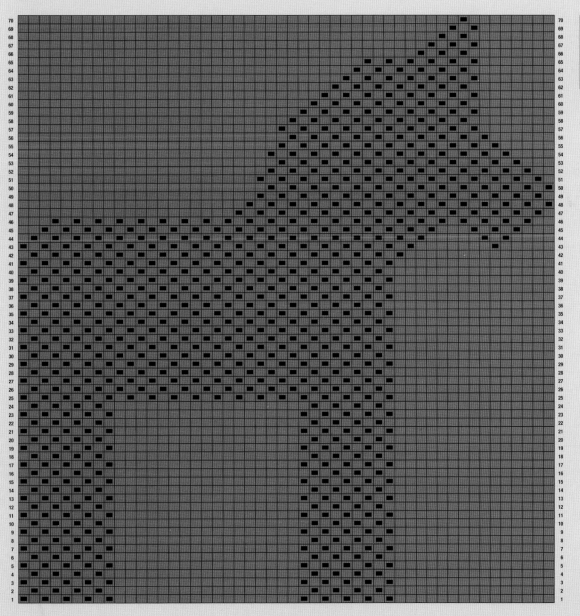

Dala Horse Sweater Chart

KEY
MC Knit
MC Purl

$\mathcal{M}$anly Mansion Muffler

Finished Measurements
Width: 7"/18cm
Length: 52"/132cm

Materials

- Blackberry Ridge Natural Colored, 100% Wool Yarn, 4oz/113g, 350yds/320m:
- Dark Grey (MC) and Brown (CC), 1 skein each
- Size 8 (5mm), 36"/91.5cm long circular needles or size needed to obtain gauge (2)
- Tapestry needle

Gauge
14 sts and 20 rows = 4"/10cm.
Adjust needle size as necessary to obtain correct gauge.

The stonework at the American Swedish Institute inspired this cozy scarf, which replicates the big and little repeat design in the mansion's limestone block pattern. The scarf is knit using the double-knitting technique, not to be confused with dk weight yarn! Although this muffler was designed for a man, it would be perfect for the contemporary woman as well. Choose the Blackberry Ridge yarn we used (a slightly "toothy" natural-colored wool) or a slick, soft merino and this pattern will be a great layer for your winter wearing! Our thanks go out to Nancy Lindberg, from whom we learned this technique, and to Debbie Stoller, for making it hip again.

Special Techniques
Crochet Cast-On (see Special Techniques Used, page 140)

Pattern Notes
Double knitting is working both sides in one row. The chart represents the side facing you. For each square there is a knit stitch for the side facing you of the color indicated on the chart and a purl stitch for the other

side in the opposite color. Therefore each stitch is really two stitches—one front stitch in knit and one back stitch in purl.

At the beginning of each row you will need to twist the two colors to close each end.

Instructions

Using crochet cast-on method and MC, CO 362 sts (multiple of 60 + 2).

Set-Up Row: (K1 MC, p1 CC) across row.

Using stranded method of choice, beginning with Chart Row 1, sl first st; *with both colors in back, k the st in color indicated on chart; with both colors in front, p the back st in opposite color; rep from * across each st on chart to last st; with both colors in front, p last st with both colors. Cont working in double knitting, rep Chart Rows 1–17 twice.

BO Row: *With MC, k1, p1 and pass first st over second st to BO; rep from * across row.

FINISHING

Weave in ends.

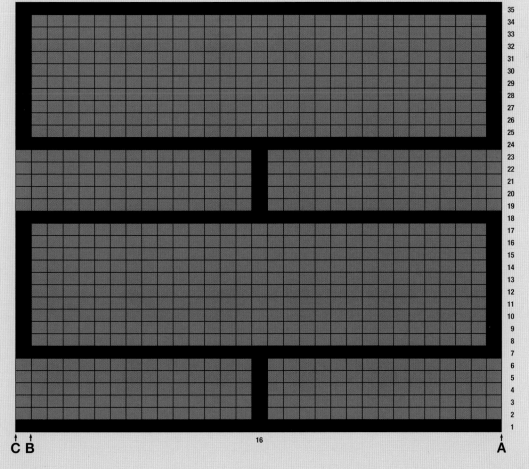

Manly Mansion Muffler Chart

KEY

K on RS, P on WS

K on RS, P on WSI

Note: In double knitting, charts show only the RS of the pattern, but remember that each box on the chart actually represents two stitches: the right side as shown and the "hidden" back side. Once you've knit the RS stitch in the color shown, remember to purl the WS stitch in the opposite color.

CHAPTER 3

Two-Color Knitting

Spinning wool in Sweden, 1914.
AMERICAN SWEDISH INSTITUTE COLLECTION

The Swedes and Norwegians may have been rivals, but in this section we celebrate their shared knitting traditions. These designs feature knitting techniques that are popular in both countries, including the stranded, two-color variety. Norway and Sweden also share motifs like the snowflake and star that appear in our Swedish Mittens design.

Piper's Hat

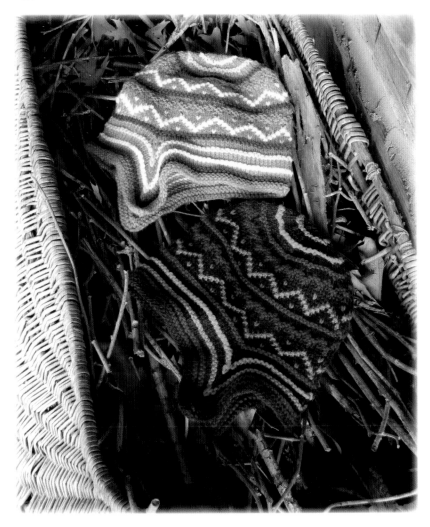

Size
Adult's Average

Finished Measurements
Circumference: 20"/51cm
Height: 12"/30.5cm (from top
of hat to tip of earflap)

Materials

- Cascade 220, 100% wool,
  100g/3.5oz, 220yds/201m:
- *New Deal version*: Pink
  Heather #2451 (MC), Light
  Blue #7816 (A), Navy #7818
  (B), White, #8505 (C), Gold
  #8412 (D), 1 skein each
- *Modern version*: Purple
  #7803 (MC), Teal #9421
  (A), Navy #7818 (B), Light
  Blue #7816, Shrek #8903
  (D), 1 skein each
- Size 7 (4.5mm), 16"/40.5cm
  long circular needle or size
  needed to obtain gauge
- Size 7 (4.5mm) double-
  pointed needles
- Stitch markers (4)
- Safety pins (2)
- Tapestry needle

Gauge
18 sts and 22 rnds = 4"/10cm
in St st.
*Adjust needle size as neces-
sary to obtain correct gauge.*

In the 1930s, Evelyn Paulson embroidered a depiction of a Swedish bridal procession onto a long piece of linen fabric. The scene includes a wedding party with people in folk costumes. This wall hanging, a WPA handcraft project, was part of FDR's New Deal to support the arts. This particular piece hung in the Bridgeview School in St. Paul, Minnesota, and was donated to the ASI by Donna Flug in 1984.

The colors used in this wall hanging are indicative of the Depression era, a time when people used the materials that were available to them because resources were very limited. The New Deal version of the hat is knit with the traditional colors used in the original embroidered piece. The Modern version of the hat is made using more contemporary colors. Both color combinations are fun to make and wear.

Special Abbreviations

S2KP2: Slip 2 sts tog knitwise, k1, pass the slipped sts over (this is a centered double dec).

Pattern Notes

The hat is constructed in one piece, including the earflaps. The earflaps are formed by a centered double decrease on each side of the hat. Note that the earflaps are set toward the back of the hat and not centered, to provide better coverage over the ears.

Instructions

With MC, CO 148 sts. Pm for beg of rnd and join, taking care not to twist sts.

Rnd 1: Knit.

Rnd 2: Purl.

Rnd 3: Attach A; knit, placing safety pin in the 31st and 118th sts to mark the center dec for each earflap.

Rnd 4: With A, purl.

Rnd 5: *With MC, k to 1 st before marked st; S2KP2; rep from * once, k to end—144 sts.

Rnd 6: *With B, k to 1 st before marked st; S2KP2; rep from * once, k to end—140 sts.

Rnd 7: *With B, p to 1 st before marked st; S2KP2;. rep from * once, p to end—136 sts.

Rnds 8–9: *With MC, k to 1 st before marked st; S2KP2; rep from * once, k to end—128 sts.

Rnd 10: *With C, k to 1 st before marked st; S2KP2; rep from * once, k to end—124 sts.

Rnd 11: *With C, p to 1 sts before marked st; 2SKP2; rep from * once, p to end—120 sts.

Swedish Bridal Embroidery by Evelyn Paulson.
AMERICAN SWEDISH
INSTITUTE COLLECTION

Rnds 12–14: *With MC, k to 1 st from marked st; S2KP2; rep from * once, k to end—108 sts.

Rnd 15: *With D, k to 1 st before marked st; S2KP2; rep from * once, k to end—104 sts.

Rnd 16: *With D, p to 1 sts before marked st; S2KP2; rep from * once, p to end—100 sts.

Rnds 17–19: *With MC, k to 1 st before marked st; S2KP2; rep from * once, k to end—88 sts.

Rnds 20–33: Foll Chart A on 88 sts.

Rnds 34–47: Foll Chart B; on the last rnd of chart; work S2KP2 between every other zigzag pat as indicated—66 sts.

TOP DEC RNDS

Rnd 1: *With B, knit.

Rnd 2: With B, purl.

Rnds 3–5: With MC, knit.

Rnd 6: With D, *S2KP, k3; rep from * around—44 sts.

Rnd 7: With D, purl.

Rnds 8–10: With MC, knit.

Rnd 11: With C, *S2KP, k1; rep from * around—22 sts.

Rnds 12–14: With MC, knit.

Rnd 15: K2tog around—11 sts.

Break yarn, leaving a 6"/15cm tail. Using tapestry needle, thread tail thru rem sts, pull tight, and secure ends.

FINISHING

Weave in all ends. Block.

Piper's Hat Charts

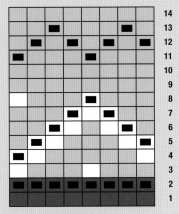

CHART A

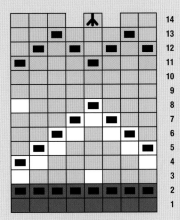

CHART B

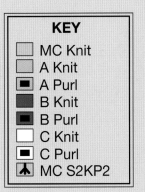

KEY

☐	MC Knit
☐	A Knit
◼	A Purl
◼	B Knit
◼	B Purl
☐	C Knit
◼	C Purl
⅄	MC S2KP2

Deer Mittens

Size
Adult's Large

Finished Measurements
Circumference: 8 ¼"/21cm
Length: 10 ½"/26.5cm

Materials

- Klippan/Cum Ullgarn 7/2, 100% wool, 100g/3.5oz, 340yds/311m: Blue (MC) and Green (CC), 1 skein each
- **Note**: If this yarn is not available, substitute with Reynolds Whiskey, 100% wool, 50g/1.75oz, 195yds/178m.
- Size 0 (2 mm) and 2 (2.75 mm) double-pointed needles or size needed to obtain gauge
- Stitch markers (one in CC for beg of rnd)
- Waste yarn or stitch holder
- Tapestry needle

Gauge
34 sts and 40 rnds = 4"/10 cm in stranded two-color St st on larger needles.
Adjust needle size as necessary to obtain correct gauge.

This mitten design is based on a brown and cream glove in the ASI collection. The original gloves, donated by Ruth Sandberg Nelson, were knit in 1920 by Sara Wahlstrom, Ruth's grandmother. The deer motif has a free-form and "organic" style, which differentiates it from other more common deer designs found in commercial two-color knitting. The upside-down opposing deer solves the problem of which direction to place the motifs on the mitten: Are the mittens viewed with hands down or hands up? In this case it does not matter.

Pattern Notes

- After working the cuff, follow the chart throughout and shape as indicated.
- The colorwork is done using the "stranded" method, carrying both colors at once. Avoid long floats on the inside of the mitten in those areas where more than five consecutive stitches are worked in one color by catching the color not in use with the working color.

Instructions

CUFF

With smaller dpns and MC, CO 64 sts. Pm at beg of rnd and join, taking care not to twist sts.

Rnds 1–20: Work 20 rnds of k1, p1 corrugated ribbing as foll: *K1 MC, yf CC, p1 CC, yb CC; rep from * around.

Rnd 21: Knit with MC, inc 8 sts evenly spaced—72 sts.

Rnd 22: Purl, with MC.

Change to larger dpns.

MAIN MITTEN

Rnds 1–21: Foll Chart A, Rnds 1–21.

THUMB OPENING

Left Mitten—Rnd 22: Working Chart A, Rnd 22, work 19 sts, k next 17 sts with waste yarn, slip these sts back to left needle, cont in pat.

Right Mitten—Rnd 22: Working Chart A, Rnd 22, k3, k next 17 sts onto waste yarn, slip these sts back to left needle, cont in pat.

BOTH MITTENS

Cont to foll Chart A to beg of shaping.

Decrease Set-Up: Pm after first 3 sts, pm after next 33 sts, pm after next 3 sts, pm after last 33 sts.

Cont to work to top of Chart A working decs every rnd sixteen times as foll:

Decrease Rnd: K3, slm (slip marker), ssk, k to within 2 sts of next marker, k2tog, slm, k3, slm, ssk, k to within last 2 sts, k2tog (4 sts dec'd). Break yarn leaving a 6"/15cm tail.

With tapestry needle, thread yarn through rem sts and pull tight; secure tail on WS.

Brown and white deer motif gloves donated by Ruth Sandberg Nelson, knit in 1920 by Sara Wahlstrom, Ruth's grandmother.

OLD SWEDISH RECIPE

SWEDISH FATTIGMANDS

MAKES ABOUT 4 DOZEN COOKIES

4 egg yolks + 2 eggs

⅔ c. confectioners' sugar

½ c. heavy whipping cream

1 tbsp. brandy or cognac

1 tbsp. ground cardamom

½ tsp. grated lemon peel

½ tsp. salt

2–2 ½ c. all-purpose flour

Vegetable or canola oil for frying (at least 1 qt.)

1 c. confectioners' sugar mixed with a 1 tsp. ground cardamom for dusting

Candy thermometer

In a large bowl, beat egg yolks and confectioners' sugar for 10 minutes, or until thick and light lemon colored. Add additional eggs and beat to blend. Stir in whipping cream, brandy or cognac, cardamom, lemon peel, and salt. Mix in enough flour to make a stiff dough. Cover and chill at least three hours.

In a heavy pan, heat oil (at least 4 inches deep) to 375°F. Put candy thermometer in place to monitor temperature.

Meanwhile, on a well-floured board, divide the dough in half and roll very thinly (⅛ inch). If the dough is sticking, gradually add more flour. With a pizza cutter, or fattigmand cutter, cut dough one way, then the other, to form diamonds about 2 ½x3 inches (exact dimensions don't really matter). In the center of each diamond, form a ¾-inch slit. Pick up each piece and insert one end of the diamond into the slit; pull partway through to form a knot.

Fry in small batches in the 375°F oil (adjusting your stove burner to keep the oil at temperature) for about 15 seconds on a side, until golden brown. Remove with a slotted spoon or spider to a paper-towel-covered cookie sheet to drain. Sprinkle with cardamom-laced powdered sugar while still hot.

Smaklig måltid! (Enjoy the meal!)

THUMB

Remove waste yarn and place the 17 sts onto needle, pm, pick up additional 17 sts around back of thumb opening—34 sts.

Foll Thumb Chart to beg of shaping.

Cont to work to top of Thumb Chart, working decs every rnd eight times as foll:

Decreases: SSK, k to within 2 sts of next marker, k2tog, k2, ssk, k to within last 2 sts, ssk.

Break off yarn, leaving a 6"/15cm tail.

With tapestry needle, thread yarn through rem sts and pull tight; secure tail on WS.

FINISHING

Weave in all ends. Block.

Deer Mittens Charts

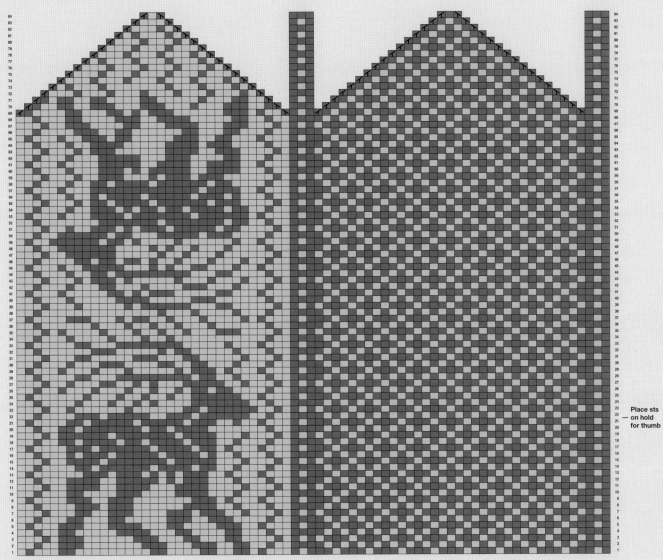

Place sts on hold for thumb

CHART A

THUMB CHART

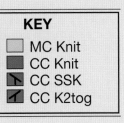

KEY

☐	MC Knit
■	CC Knit
◪	CC SSK
◪	CC K2tog

Hilma's Gloves

Size
Adult's Medium

Finished Measurements
Circumference: 7 ½"/19cm
Length: 11"/28cm (can be
adjusted based on finger
length)

Materials

- Nature Spun Fingering by
  Brown Sheep, 100% wool,
  50g/1.75oz/310 yds/283m;
  Aran #N91 (MC), Scarlet
  #N48 (A), Evergreen #N24
  (B), 1 skein each
- Off-white (MC), Red (A),
  Forest (B), 1 skein each
- Size 1 (2.25mm) double-
  pointed needles (set of 5) or
  size needed to obtain gauge
- Waste yarn or stitch holder
- Stitch markers (one CC for
  beg of rnd)
- Tapestry needle

Gauge
48 sts and 44 rows = 4"/10cm
in stranded 2-color St st.
Adjust needle size as neces-
sary to obtain correct gauge.

These gloves are named after Hilma Berglund, daughter of Swedish immigrants and co-founder of the Minnesota Weaver's Guild. The repeating pattern was inspired by Hilma's notebook, which contains many graphs and notes on weaving patterns. The weaving pattern has been knit vertically in three colors to create optical striping along the length of the glove. The saying "One life isn't enough for all the things I'd like to do" is a quote from Hilma's journal and is very appropriate for any fiber artist.

Pattern Notes

The pattern is written for the right glove, which contains the quote. The left glove can be made with only the repeating pattern, the quote, or create your own special message.

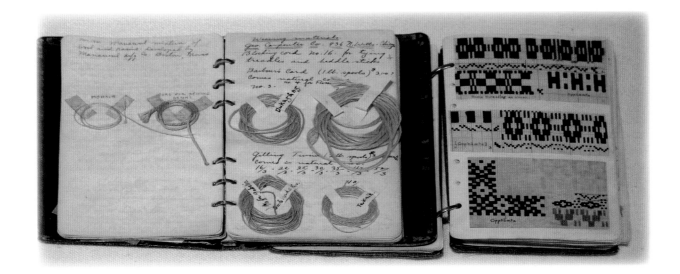

Instructions

With MC, CO 88 sts, distributed evenly on 4 dpns. Pm for beg of rnd and join, taking care not to twist sts.

MAIN GLOVE

Rnds 1–53: Join A and foll Chart A, joining B as needed.

THUMB OPENING

Right Glove—Rnd 54: With waste yarn k22 sts; slip these back to left needle, then cont Rnd 54 as charted.

Left Glove—Rnd 54: K22 sts, k22 sts with waste yarn, then cont Rnd 54 as charted.

BOTH GLOVES—CENTER HAND SECTION

Rnds 55–82: Cont to foll Chart A.

POINTER FINGER

Rnd 83: Foll Pointer Chart, work 11 sts; place next 66 sts onto a stitch holder; CO 10 sts in pat placing marker in middle of CO sts; then work rem 11 sts—32 sts.

Cont to foll Pointer Chart until ½"/13mm from desired length.

Pointer Finger Tip Decreases

Dec Rnd: K1, ssk, k to 3 sts from marker, k2tog, k1.

Rep dec rnd until 8 sts rem.

Break off yarn, leaving a 6"/15cm tail.

With tapestry needle, thread rem sts and pull tight; secure end on WS.

We drew inspiration for Hilma's Gloves straight from the pages of her weaving journal from the pattern she called Opphämta.
AMERICAN SWEDISH INSTITUTE COLLECTION

MIDDLE FINGER

Place 22 sts from front and 11 sts from back onto needles; pick up and k10 sts in pat along CO edge from Pointer Finger, placing SOR marker in middle of 10 pick-up sts; k11 sts in pat, CO 6 sts in pat, placing marker in middle of CO sts; k11 sts in pat. Foll Middle Finger Chart until ½"/12mm from desired length.

Middle Finger Tip Decreases

Dec Rnd: K1, ssk, k to 3 sts from marker, k2tog, k1.
Rep dec rnd until 8 sts rem and finish as for Pointer Finger Tip.

RING FINGER

Place 22 sts from front and 11 sts from back onto needles; pick-up and k6 sts in pat along CO edge from Middle Finger placing SOR marker in middle of pick-up sts; k11 sts in pat; CO 4 sts in pat placing marker in middle of CO sts; k11 sts in pat. Foll Middle Finger Chart until ½"/12mm from desired length.

Ring Finger Tip Decreases

Decrease Rnd: K1, ssk, k to 3 sts from marker, k2tog, k1.
Rep dec rnd until 8 sts rem and finish as for Pointer Finger Tip.

PINKY FINGER

Place rem 22 sts on needles; pick up and k4 sts in pat along CO edge from Ring Finger, placing SOR marker in middle of pick-up sts.
Foll Pinky Chart until ½"/12mm from desired length.

Pinky Finger Tip Decreases

Decrease Rnd: K1, ssk, k to 3 sts from marker, k2tog, k1.
Rep dec rnd until 8 sts rem and finish as for Pointer Finger Tip.

THUMB

Remove waste yarn and place live upper sts and lower sts on needles—44 sts.
Attach yarns and follow Thumb Chart until 1"/2.5cm from desired length. Pm after 22nd st.
Dec Rnd: K1, ssk, k to 3 sts from marker, k2tog, k1.
Rep dec rnd until 8 sts rem and finish as for Pointer Finger Tip.

FINISHING

Weave in all ends. Block.

Weaving Hilma's Story

Hilma Berglund collecting birch bark for natural dying near her family cabin, called "Two Pines," on Lake Pokegama, near Pine City, Minnesota.
AMERICAN SWEDISH INSTITUTE COLLECTION

Hilma Berglund (1886–1972) was a tirelessly inquisitive and creative artist who devoted her life to the study and practice of textile crafts. Her work and her words leave behind an engaging portrait of her talent and enthusiasm.

Hilma was born in Stillwater, Minnesota, to Swedish immigrant parents. As a child, Hilma suffered from migraine headaches, and consequently, she was taken out of school. She took up art to occupy herself during her convalescence at home, experimenting with embroidery, china painting, pottery, and photography. Later, she began her formal training at the St. Paul School of Art.

A wise woman, she used her income frugally to travel and learn about fiber traditions from each country she visited. She had many talented and influential friends whom she often visited and traveled with. Hilma's interest in the arts is recorded in her journals and demonstrated by the many handcrafted objects she collected.

On a 1914 trip to Sweden, she discovered the Johanna BrunssonVävskola, a school established to preserve and perpetuate the fine hand-weaving traditions of Sweden. Soon after she enrolled, World War II broke

out, so Hilma hastily wove a towel sampler that was, in the words of her instructor, Miss Brunsson, "more suited for dish cloths," and returned to St. Paul.

In 1922, Hilma returned to Stockholm and enrolled at HandarbetetsVännerVävskola. This time she was able to attend classes and wove many samplers using traditional Swedish weaving techniques. Fortunately, Hilma was fluent in Swedish, and she was allowed to take their weave theory classes. The hours of lessons are recorded in her notebooks, written in both English and Swedish. Hilma noted, "People in Scandinavia are textile conscious. If they themselves do not weave, they buy handwoven fabrics to serve their needs." While at the school, she had a floorloom shipped home to St. Paul. It was soon joined by a tapestry loom, built to duplicate one she used at the Vävskola.

She continued her studies at the Handicraft Guild in Minneapolis, the Minneapolis School of Art, and the University of Minnesota, where she received a Master's degree in 1939. Hilma shared the knowledge she gained from these classes with her students and in numerous articles she wrote. She joined the Art Department at the University of Minnesota in 1930 and taught there until 1954. In 1940, Hilma co-founded the Weavers Guild of Minnesota, where she served three terms as president.

Hilma often experimented with weaving techniques and yarn combinations. One of her greatest pursuits was the use of natural dyes from plant materials that grew near her northern Minnesota cabin and in the garden of her St. Paul house. Hilma conducted numerous natural dying experiments. She used the Munsell color system—grading each fiber on its hue, value, and color purity. Much like a research scientist, she documented each sample with detailed information on the process used to achieve the colors. A booklet of Hilma's work with natural dyes was published posthumously.

She summed up her inquisitive attitude in a 1966 Christmas letter, in which she described a trip to the Midwest Weavers' Conference: "Why do I go? I am always interested in weaving and . . . trends which are different from any I have seen before."

Special thanks to Phyllis Waggoner for providing historical information on Hilma Berglund.

Hilma's Gloves Charts

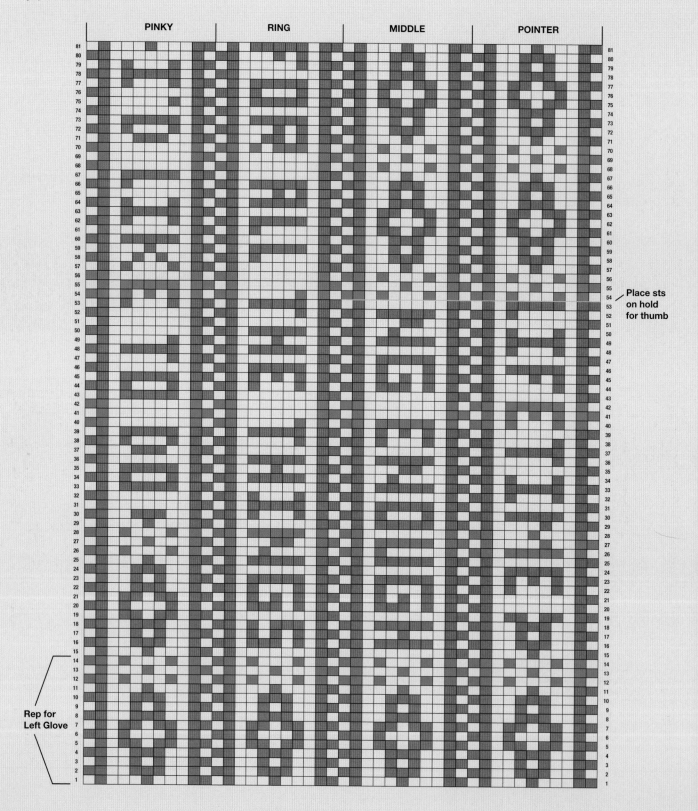

PINKY   RING   MIDDLE   POINTER

Place sts on hold for thumb

Rep for Left Glove

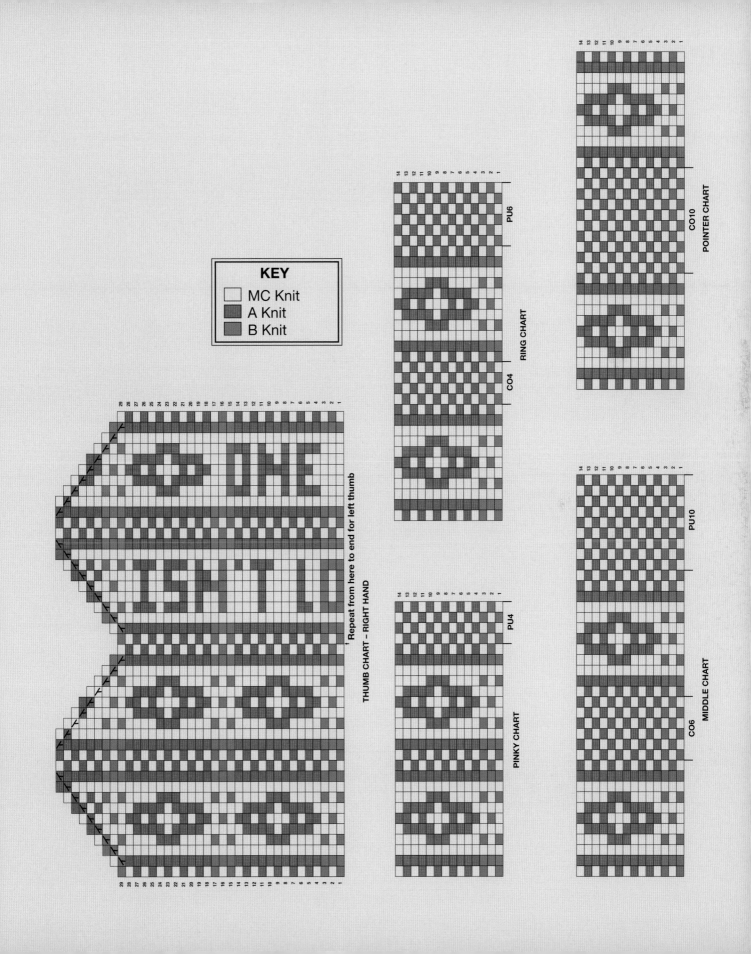

KEY

☐ MC Knit
▨ A Knit
▨ B Knit

† Repeat from here to end for left thumb

THUMB CHART – RIGHT HAND

RING CHART

PU6

CO4

POINTER CHART

CO10

PINKY CHART

PU4

MIDDLE CHART

PU10

CO6

Size

Sweater is meant to be worn as a jacket and has one size. To make garment smaller or larger, adjust your gauge in Stockinette stitch and follow pattern.

Finished Measurements

Bust: 54"/137cm
Length: 26"/66cm

Materials

- Classic Elite Yarns Liberty Wool 100% washable wool, 50g/1.75oz, 122yds/112m:
- Deep Teal #7846 (MC), 16 skeins
- Gold #7850 (CC), 4 skeins
- Size 8 (5mm), 32"/81.5cm long circular needle or size needed to obtain gauge
- Size 7 (4.5mm), 32"/81.5cm long circular needle (or 1 size smaller than size needed to obtain gauge)
- Size 7 (4.5mm) double-pointed needles (or 1 size smaller than size needed to obtain gauge)
- Stitch markers (2)
- Coilless pin-style stitch marker (1)
- Buttons (9)
- Tapestry needle

Gauge

20 sts and 24 rows = 4"/10cm in St st on larger needles. *Adjust needle size as necessary to obtain correct gauge.*

Hope Chest Sweater

This sweater crosses the border between Norway and Sweden. It is a marriage of Swedish-influenced weaving motifs and Norwegian knitting styles and techniques. We wanted to include items inspired by weaving in this collection, so when we found this piece of woven yardage, we knew we were on to something. The original yardage was woven by Silma Birch in 1905 for her hope chest. We assume it was in preparation for coming to America. The fabric is linen, spun from flax raised on her family farm. The original fabric is so beautiful, it's no wonder Silma never cut into it! We modeled the color pattern for this sweater after Silma's woven yardage. The solid section is created using a knitting motif that looks like weaving.

Special Techniques

Cable Cast-On (see Special Techniques Used, page 140)
Three-Needle Bind-Off (see Special Techniques used, page 140)

Woven yardage attributed to Silma Birch in 1905. It is said that the flax used to weave the yardage was from her family farm in Sweden.
AMERICAN SWEDISH INSTITUTE COLLECTION

Two-Stitch One-Row Buttonhole: *Sl 1 purlwise, pass first slipped st over second st; rep from * once. Place last st back on left needle, turn. Using cable cast-on method, CO 3 sts, turn, sl next st to right needle, and pass the extra CO st over the slipped st.

Pattern Stitches

Mock Cable Ribbing (multiple of 4 + 2—see chart)
Basketweave Pattern (multiple of 18 + 10—see chart)
Transition Checkerboard Pattern (multiple of 4 + 2—see chart)
Large-Weave Stranded Pattern (multiple of 18 + 7—see chart)

Instructions

With MC and smaller needle, CO 270 sts. Join, being careful not to twist sts.
Rnd 1 (RS): K2, pm, beg Row 1 of Mock Cable Ribbing Chart (multiple of 4 sts + 2), working to 4 sts before marker, pm, k2.
Note: The 4 sts between markers are your steek sts. Beg of rnd is between these sts.
Cont to k the 4 steek sts and foll Mock Cable Ribbing pat for 2 ¼"/5.5cm or 8 reps.

BASKETWEAVE PATTERN (MULTIPLE OF 18 + 10)

Knit 1 rnd, inc 10 sts evenly around—280 sts.
Change to larger needle, rep Basketweave pat for four and a half times or for 10 ¼"/26cm, keeping steek sts as est.

TRANSITION CHECKERBOARD PATTERN (MULTIPLE OF 4 + 2)

With CC, work 4 rnds in garter st, inc 1 st each end of the 1st rnd once after and once before steek sts—282 sts.
Work Transition Checkerboard Chart once, keeping steek sts as est.
With MC work 4 rnds in garter st, dec 1 st in the 1st rnd, after steek sts—281 sts.

LARGE-WEAVE STRANDED PATTERN (MULTIPLE OF 18 + 7)

Work Large-Weave Stranded Chart Rows 1–32 once, then Rows 1–27 once, keeping steek sts as est.

Place all sts on a holder for body of sweater. Weave in ends.

SLEEVE (MAKE 2)

With MC, and dpns, CO 48 sts. Pm at beg of rnd and join, being careful not to twist sts.

Work Mock Cable Ribbing for 2 ¼"/5.5cm or 8 reps, ending with Row 2.

Inc Row: K 1 rnd inc 1 st—49 sts.

Place coilless pin-style st marker on the 1st st.

Note: All incs will be done after the marked st at the beg of the rnd and before the marked st at the end of the rnd.

Rep Basketweave pat seven and a half times, ending on Row 9; at the same time inc every 3rd rnd, ending with a total of 139 sts.

SLEEVE FACING

Work last rnd of sleeve to the last 2 sts, k2tog (these last 2 sts should include the center st). Beg working back and forth in Rev St st with MC. To personalize your sweater, chart the recipient's name in the sleeve facing using the instructions in the Alphabet Sleeve Facing sidebar on page 65.

Row 1 (RS): Purl.

Row 2: K1, M1, k to last st, M1, k1.

Row 3: P1, M1, p to last st, M1, p1.

Rep Rows 2 and 3 twice more.

BO. Weave in ends.

CUT NECK

On front of sweater, mark off 40 sts on each side of neck for shoulders. Mark neck depth of 3"/7.5cm. Using a piece of cotton waste yarn, baste the shape of neckline around front of sweater. With machine, sew along the marked neck twice and cut out crescent, leaving ¾"/2cm seam allowance.

CUT CARDIGAN FRONT AND ARMHOLES

Using a contrasting color of cotton yarn, baste one line from side marker to marked armhole depth position, going between 2 center side edge sts, and another line down front of sweater between the 4 steek sts. (See Marking, Sewing, and Cutting a Steek for Sleeves on page 66. After sewing in sleeves, loosely sew facing to WS of armhole, covering cut edge.

NECKBAND

With RS facing, using MC and smaller needle, pick up and k32 sts along right neck edge, k62 sts of back neck, pick up and k32 sts along left neck edge—126 sts. *Do not join.*

Work in Mock Cable Ribbing for 4 reps.

TURNING ROW AND FACING

**Row 1 (RS): Purl.

Row 2 (WS): Purl.

Row 3: Knit.

Rep Rows 2 and 3 three more times.

Rep Row 1.
BO.**
Using MC, loosely sew facing to WS of neck, covering cut edge.
Join shoulders, using three-needle BO.

LEFT FRONT BUTTON BAND

With RS facing, using MC, smaller needle, and pick-up method "3 sts for every 4 rows" or "2 sts for every 3 sts," pick up and k114 sts along Left Front edge for button band. Work Mock Cable Ribbing for 4 reps.
Rep from ** to ** on Neckband once for turning row and facing.

RIGHT FRONT BUTTONHOLE BAND

Using same pick-up method as for button band, pick up and k114 sts along Right Front edge for buttonhole band. Work Mock Cable Ribbing for 1 rep, ending with a WS row.

Buttonhole Row: Work 8 sts in pat, *work Two-st Buttonhole (see Special Techniques), work 10 sts in pat, rep from * for a total of nine buttonholes.

Note: The placement of buttonholes is divided equally by two and a half MC reps.

Work 2 reps of Mock Cable Ribbing for a total of 4 reps, ending with a WS row.

Rep from ** to ** on Neckband once for turning row and facing.

FINISHING

Using MC, loosely sew facing to WS of fronts, covering cut edge. Sew on buttons.

Weave in all ends. Block facings and bands.

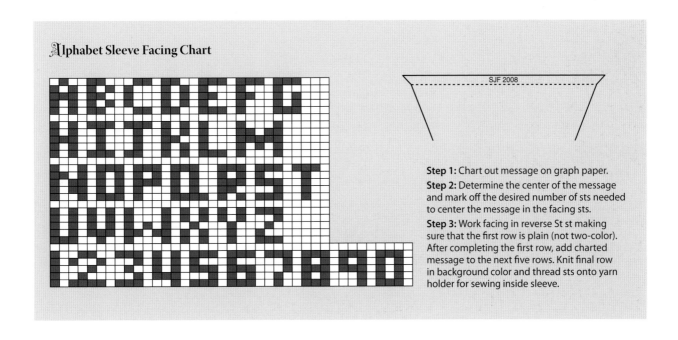

Alphabet Sleeve Facing Chart

SJF 2008

Step 1: Chart out message on graph paper.

Step 2: Determine the center of the message and mark off the desired number of sts needed to center the message in the facing sts.

Step 3: Work facing in reverse St st making sure that the first row is plain (not two-color). After completing the first row, add charted message to the next five rows. Knit final row in background color and thread sts onto yarn holder for sewing inside sleeve.

Marking, Sewing, and Cutting a Steek for Sleeves

Marking Armhole

Cutting Armhole

Step 1: Measure the diameter of the sleeve at the turning ridge before the facing. Mark the armhole depth on the body based on this measurement. Use a contrasting piece of cotton yarn to baste a line between the two center underarm stitches from the side marker (still on the needle) to the bottom of the armhole; make sure to clearly mark the bottom of the armhole. This basting yarn will be your cutting line.

Step 2: Thread the sewing machine with a contrasting thread and set the machine to small stitches. Place the knitting under the machine foot and begin to sew, slowly moving the basted armhole forward; do not allow the fabric to pucker. Stitch on top of the knitted stitches *adjacent to* the basting yarn, going from the shoulder to the bottom of the armhole; turn, sew across bottom stitches of the armhole, then sew back up on the top of the knitted stitches *adjacent to* the other side of the basting thread. You should have a long, narrow "U" machine-stitched around the basting yarn. Try to avoid sewing in the "ditch," or over the bars between the stitches, since this does not catch enough of the fiber for a strong steek.

NOTE: Some knitters prefer to sew the shoulder seam together at this point to prepare the garment for sewing in the sleeves. This will minimize any extra handling of the garment once the sleeve opening is cut. The raw stitches will be exposed for a shorter time than if the shoulder seam is joined after the cutting.

Step 3: Cut along the basting yarn to open up the armhole. Sew the sleeve into place 1–2 stitches from the cut edge on each side, attaching the sleeve along the first row of the facing.

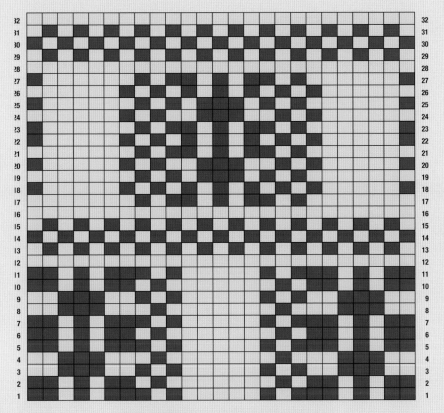

Large Weave Multiple of 18 + 7

	KEY
•	CC Purl
▢	CC Knit
▨	MC Knit
•	MC Purl
⌣	Over 2 sts-wyb, sl1 p-wise, yo, K1, psso both sts

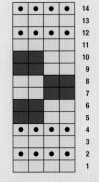

**Transition Checkerboard
Multiple of 4 sts**

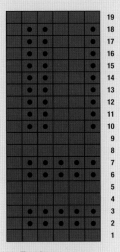

**Basketweave
Multiple of 6 sts**

**Mock Cable Ribbing
Multiple of 4 + 2**

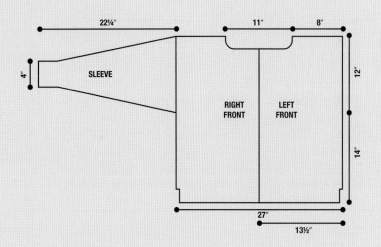

What Came before Knitting: Nålbindning

By Kate Martinson

Surely when we picture Sweden many images come to mind, among them patterned knitted items of remarkable beauty and character. This knitting, *stickning*, is so important that assumptions are often made about the invention of knitting in Sweden or its Scandinavian neighbors, or the extreme length of time knitting has been in use in that area.

The first knitted items we find in Sweden date from around 1566 in King Eric of Sweden's inventory of silk socks. Over time knitting filtered down to lower classes, even becoming a popular trade item from Sweden in the eighteenth and nineteenth centuries.

There were a number of techniques for textile production that predated knitting, but the one that functions most like knitting is a sewn single horizontal interlooped technique called *nålbindning, binda med nål* or *nåla* in Swedish (versus vertically interlooped *stickning* made with two needles). Variations of this technique appear worldwide and in some of the earliest human habitation sites, including in the frozen north. A single-eyed needle, *nål*, can be used to create a fabric that can vary in shape, density, and elasticity. The fabric created does not unravel when worn or cut, so it is perfect for the hardiest of work clothes such as mittens for fishermen and foresters, yet also works for finely made ribbons and mittens with detailed floral embroidery. *Nål* were used to make everything from sieves and horse blankets to hairy toecaps that tied on leather shoes in icy conditions. In fact, when knitting was first done in Sweden and other parts of Scandinavia, it mimicked *nålbindning* in the distinctive shape of knitted objects like gloves and mittens and the practice of embroidered surfaces that were later replaced by the iconic stranded patterns.

Nålbindning lasted much longer in Sweden than it did in other Scandinavian countries. When textile historian Lilli Zick Letterman began her study, organization, and preservation of folk handwork in the late 1800s, this would have been one of many techniques of interest to her. *Nålbindning* was still used and passed along as part of an oral tradition, too lowly to require printed directions. Early craft preservation vehicles such as the *Svensk Hemslojd* (Society of Swedish Handicrafts), schools, and museums continued to preserve *nålbindning* into the 1970s, when publishing and classes helped to bring the technique into the twenty-first century, where it is shared and practiced internationally with renewed vigor.

This pair of black mittens, made with the "needle looping" technique, is decorated with wool crewel embroidery in the Darlana style.
DONOR UNKNOWN, AMERICAN SWEDISH INSTITUTE COLLECTION

Traveler's-Inspired Sweater

A number of years ago, we had the pleasure of inviting our friend, Jean Christensen, to our knitting group to teach a class on the Traveling Sweater. The concept of the traveling sweater was first described in the 1985 Fall/Winter issue of *Knitter's* magazine.

Basically, the sweater is constructed using your favorite colors, striped against a neutral background. Since the sweater contains all of the colors you are likely to have in your wardrobe, this sweater is the only one you'll need to pack on your next trip, hence the name "traveler's sweater."

In this particular pattern, the colors are drawn from a beautiful, hand-woven skirt that is part of a provincial folk costume purchased for Irene S. Anderson by her father in 1946. The garter stitch stripes in the *Knitter's* version of the traveling sweater have been replaced with the patterns that were found in the skirt, which is from the area of Skåne, Sweden. In Skåne, women were sure to wear at least two skirts so they could use the top one to cover their heads if it started raining.

Sizes
Woman's Small (Medium, Large, X-Large)

Finished Measurements:
Chest: 34 (38, 42, 46)"/85 (95, 105, 115)cm
Length: 22 ¼ (23 ¼, 24 ½, 25 ¾)"/55.5 (58, 61, 65.5)cm

Materials

- Cascade 220 Sport, 100% wool, 50g/1.75oz, 164yds/150m:
- **Olive/Rust Colorway**: Bittersweet #7824 (MC) and Cream #8010 (A), 3 skeins each
- Black #8555 (C) and Rust #2414 (D), 2 skeins each
- Olive #2452 (B) and Yellow #4147 (E), 1 skein each
- **Swedish Blues Colorway**: Medium Blue #9456 (MC), 5 skeins
- Cream #8010 (A), 3 skeins
- Dark Blue #7818 (C), 2 skeins
- Light Blue #8905 (B) and Yellow #4147 (D), 1 skein each
- Sizes 4 (3.5mm) and 6 (4mm) double-pointed needles and 24"/60cm long circular needles or size needed to obtain gauge
- Buttons (8)
- Waste yarn or stitch holders
- Stitch markers
- Tapestry needle

Gauge
26 sts and 28 rows = 4"/10cm in St st on larger needles.
Adjust needle size, as needed to obtain correct gauge.

Special Techniques

Applied I-cord (see Special Techniques Used, page 140)

Crochet Cast-On (see Special Techniques Used, page 140)

Kitchener Stitch (see Special Techniques Used, page 140)

Special Abbreviations

S2KP2: Slip 2 sts tog knitwise, k1, pass the slipped sts over; this is a centered double decrease.

S2PP2: Slip 2 sts tog purlwise, p1, pass the slipped sts over; this is a centered double decrease.

Pattern Notes

Each side of the sweater is constructed from the cuff to center back. The back is then Kitchener stitched down the center to join both sides. Next, a ribbing is added to the bottom of the sweater. The neckline is then picked up and worked with centered double decreases at the four neckline corners. The final touch is to work an I-cord around the front edges and back neck while working buttonholes along the way.

Instructions

RIGHT SLEEVE

With smaller dpns and A, CO 56 (60, 68, 72) sts. Pm at beg of rnd and join, taking care not to twist sts. Work in k1, p1 ribbing for 2 ½"/6cm. Change to larger dpns.

Beg foll Chart A, inc every 7, (6, 6, 6) rnds as foll: K1, M1 by lifting bar between previous sts onto left needle and k, work to end of rnd, M1. As the incs are added, maintain the est pat by compensating for the additional sts.

Cont inc until there are 112 (120, 136, 144) sts, changing to circular needle when the diameter is large enough. Work even, without incs, until sleeve measures 18 (18, 18 ½, 19)"/45 (45, 46, 47.5)cm or desired length.

BODY

At each end of underarm, using crochet cast-on with waste yarn and larger circular needle, CO 88 (92, 92, 96) sts—288 (304, 320, 336) sts.

Working back and forth in St st and maintaining est pat, work even for 4 ½ (5, 5 ¾, 6 ½)"/11 (12.5, 14, 16) cm from CO underarm edge. Pm after 144th (152nd,

160th, 168th) st to mark center top shoulder seam.

Neck opening: Place 28 (28, 28, 32) sts from center marker on waste yarn or holder for the right front neck and 12 sts after the center marker on waste yarn or holder for the back neck. **Note**: 116 (124, 132, 136) sts rem for right front; 132 (140, 148, 152) sts for left back.

RIGHT BACK

Cont in est pat in St st on re 132 (140, 148, 152) back sts until center back panel meas 4 (4 ¼, 4 ½, 4 ¾)"/10 (10.5, 11, 11.5)cm, ending with a WS row and marking pat row ended. Place these sts on waste yarn or holder.

LEFT SLEEVE

Work same as Right Sleeve until right back is completed and ending on same pat row.

Using Kitchener st, join right center back to left center back.

RIGHT FRONT

Cont in est pat in St st on rem 116 (124, 132, 136) right front sts for an additional 4 (4 ¼, 4 ½, 4 ¾)"/10 (10.5, 11, 11.5)cm. Place sts on waste yarn or holder.

LEFT FRONT

Cont in est pat in St st on rem 116 (124, 132, 136) left front sts for an additional 4 (4 ¼, 4 ½, 4 ¾)"/10 (10.5, 11, 11.5)cm. Place sts on waste yarn or holder.

JOINING SIDE SEAMS

Remove waste yarn from underarm sts and place on larger circular needle. Using Kitchener st, join side seam tog on each side.

With RS facing, using smaller circular needle and MC, pick up and k aprox 242 (250, 258, 266) sts along lower edge of sweater. Work in k1, p1 rib for 2 ½"/6cm. BO in rib.

NECK

Cont pat from where it left off on the neck sides; using the appropriate yarn color and larger circular needle, pick up and k24 (26, 28, 30) sts along the neck front, pm in corner st, k40 (40, 40, 44) sts from shoulder waste yarn or holders, pm in corner st, pick up and k48 (52, 56, 60) sts along back neck, pm in corner st, k40 (40, 40. 44) sts from shoulder waste yarn or holders, pm in corner st, pick up and k24 (26, 28, 30) sts along the neck front—176 (184, 192, 208) sts.

DECREASES

Rnd 1: *K in est pat to within 1 st of marked corner st, S2KP2; rep from * three more times, k to end (8 sts dec).

Rnd 2: *P in est pat to within 1 st of marked corner st, S2PP2; rep from * three more times, p to end (8 sts dec).

Rep Rnds 1 and 2 for 10 rows. Leave rem 96 (104, 112, 128) sts on needle for I-cord neck finish.

BUTTON BAND

With RS facing, using C and smaller dpns, starting at bottom edge right front, work applied I-cord along right front edge, around back neck, and along left front edge attaching, to the live sts. Mark for eight buttonholes evenly spaced on right front edge. With MC, work a second rnd of applied I-cord, attaching it to the first rnd of I-cord, *at buttonhole marker, work 2 rnds of unattached I-cord, skip over 2 sts on first I-cord, and then cont to work attached I-cord to the next marker, repeat from *. With MC, work a third rnd of applied I-cord, attaching it to previous rnd of I-cord. Sew buttons opposite buttonholes.

FINISHING

Weave in all ends. Block.

Hand-woven skirt from a provincial folk costume that was purchased for Irene S. Anderson by her father in 1946 from the area of Skåne, Sweden.
AMERICAN SWEDISH INSTITUTE COLLECTION

Traveler's-Inspired Sweater Charts Blue/Rust

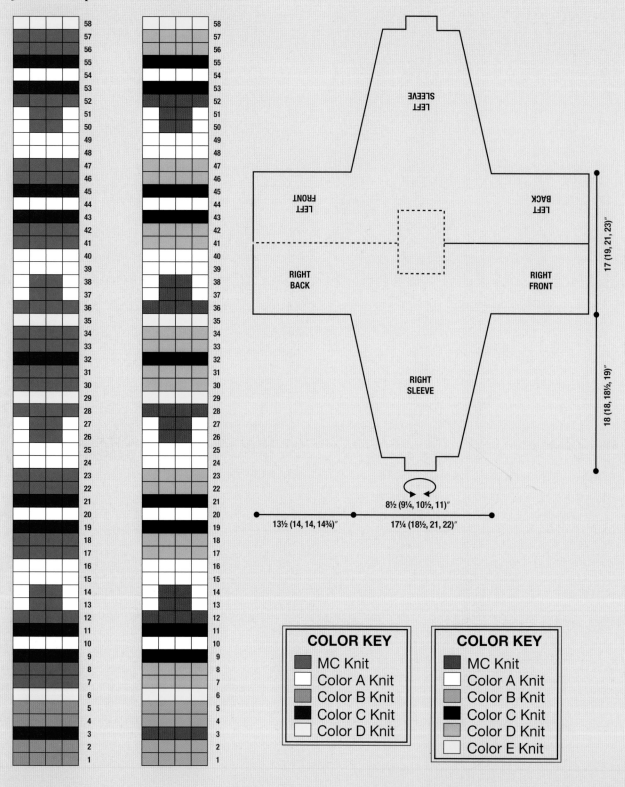

COLOR KEY

- MC Knit
- Color A Knit
- Color B Knit
- Color C Knit
- Color D Knit

COLOR KEY

- MC Knit
- Color A Knit
- Color B Knit
- Color C Knit
- Color D Knit
- Color E Knit

Carpetbags

It's impossible to enter any room at the ASI and not notice the beautifully crafted carpets. Each room contains a custom Persian-style rug that was designed exclusively for the mansion. In these two matching carpetbags, we capture the beauty of the carpets by using many of the same colors and motifs. Best of all, the bags are not difficult to knit. Imagine what other visitors to the ASI thought when they saw us on our hands and knees examining the rugs to chart the patterns. "Lose a contact?" "No, just our minds!"

Sizes

Directions are written for smaller bag with larger bag numbers in parentheses.

Finished Measurements

Small Bag: 10"/25.5cm wide by 8"/205cm high

Large Bag: 14"/35.5cm wide by 10"/25.5cm high

Materials

- Cascade 220 Heathers, 100% wool, 100g/3.5oz, 220yds/208m:
- Dark Denim Blue #2424 (MC) 2 (3) skeins
- Light Denim Blue #2423 (A), Olive #2452 (B), Rust #2425 (C), Peach #2437 (D), Yellow #2439 (E), 1 skein each
- Size 10 (6mm), 16"/40.5cm long circular and double-pointed needles or size needed to obtain gauge
- Stitch markers
- 1"/2.5cm button (1)
- Tapestry needle

Gauge

32 sts and 40 rnds = 4"/10cm in St st after felting.

Gauge is not essential for this project; just make sure your stitches are loose and airy before fulling.

The wool rug in the dining room on the first floor of the mansion was woven to complement the wood carving designs in the room. The rug includes the deep, jewel-like tones that were used in the Carpetbag designs.

Special Techniques

Applied I-cord: With dpns, CO 3 sts in MC. K2, k2tog-tbl (attaching MC I-cord to edge st from pick-up); rep along edge to end, k3tog.

Unattached I-cord: With dpns *k3, do not turn work, place right-hand needle in left hand and slip sts to other end of dpn, wrap yarn around back of work; rep from * until desired length.

Fulling (see Special Techniques Used, page 140).

Special Abbreviations

S2KP2: Slip 2 sts tog, knitwise, k1, pass the slipped sts over (this is a centered double decrease).

Pattern Stitch

SALT AND PEPPER PATTERN (S&P):

Rnd 1: *K1 A, k1 MC; rep from * around.

Rnd 2: *K1 MC, k1 A; rep from * around.

Rep Rnds 1 and 2 for pat.

Pattern Notes

Bag is worked from the opening (top) to the base (bottom). The shaping is achieved by increasing at marked corners. The base is formed by centered double decreasing at the marker corners and weaving the bottom together.

Instructions

With MC, CO 162 (250) sts. Pm for beg of rnd and join, taking care not to twist sts. Work in Garter st (k 1 rnd, p 1 rnd) for 4 rnds, pm in 1st, 63rd, 82nd, and 144th (1st, 99th, 126th, and 224th) sts for corner sts. Foll chart working an M1 inc on each side of each of the 4 marked sts every 8th rnd as indicated on chart.

Note: For accent colors in A and B in Rows 22–24, and color E in Rows 30–32 and 68–70, cut a 12"/30.5cm length of yarn for each color accent and do not carry yarn in rnd with other colors, or you can work these sts in duplicate stitch.

For Small Bag: Work chart until end of Small Bag line as indicated on the chart—218 sts.

For Large Bag: Work to top of chart—330 sts.

BASE

Rnd 1: With MC, *k1, ssk twice, k to within 4 sts from marked st, k2tog twice; rep from*, ending within 4 sts of end of rnd, k2tog twice.

Rnd 2: P, ending 1 st before end of rnd.

Note: Work base of bag in S&P pat with MC and A, always working corner sts as part of the centered double dec in MC.

Rnd 3: *S2KP2, work in S&P pat with MC and A to 1 st from marked st; rep from *, cont to work centered double decs at each corner until all sts on the short sides are consumed in the decs. Using Kitchener stitch, close the rem 86 (144 sts) with MC.

HANDLES (MAKE 2)

With MC doubled, CO 3 sts,

Row 1: K1f&b of first st, k to end.

Rows 2–5: Rep Row 1 until there are 9 sts.

Rows 6–9: Work in Garter st (k every row) for four rows.

Row 10: K2tog, k to end.

Rows 11–14: Rep Row 10 until 5 sts rem.

Handle: Work 20"/51cm I-cord on rem 5 sts as foll:

*K5, do not turn work, place right needle in left hand and slip sts to other end of needle. Wrap yarn around back of work and rep from *.

Rep Row 1 until 9 sts rem. Work four rows of Garter st. Rep Row10 until 3 sts rem, BO.

APPLIED I-CORD

Pick up purl bumps along front row of bottom, with MC and dpns, CO 3 sts. Work applied I-cord from corner to corner along bottom edge of front. Rep for back bottom edge. Work attached I-cord from the top corner down (attaching to corner sts) along side and back up to the top. Rep for second side. Work applied I-cord around top opening, at center front, working twenty rows of unattached I-cord for the button loop. Sew on button opposite button loop.

FINISHING

Weave in all ends. Full bag until it reaches finished measurements. Sew handles onto bag.

Carpetbag Chart

← No increase on last row

← End of small bag

Repeat 9 (13) times

Corner St

Repeat 3 (5) times

Corner St

Repeat Twice

COLOR KEY

- ■ MC 2424
- □ A 2423
- ▨ B 2452
- ▦ C 2425
- ▦ D 2437
- □ E 2439

Mansion Mittens

Size
Adult's Medium

Finished Measurements
Circumference: 8 ¼"/21cm
Length: 10 ½"/26.5cm

Materials

2
FINE

- Nature Spun Fingering by Brown Sheep, 100% wool, 50g/1.75oz/310 yds/283m; Spiced Plum #142 (MC) and Ash #720 (CC), 1 skein each
- Size 2 (2.75mm) double-pointed needles or size needed to obtain gauge
- Waste yarn or stitch holder
- Stitch markers (one in CC for beg of rnd)
- Tapestry needle

Gauge
34 sts and 40 rnds = 4"/10 cm in stranded two-color St st on larger needles.
Adjust needle size as necessary to obtain correct gauge.

These intricate, warm mittens encompass the very essence of the Turnblad Mansion, home to the American Swedish Institute. The basic design on the front of the mitten features the Turnblad Mansion, with its beautiful entryway and turret. The back of the mitten features the wrought iron fence that surrounds the estate. The random pattern floating in the sky is made up of symbols of various related elements—the *Posten* (the Swedish Language newspaper established by Swan Turnblad), the Swedish Flag, the Turnblad family, and so much more.

Right: Many architectural details from the mansion found their way into the Mansion Mittens design. The American Swedish Institute turret; the tall, ornate gates of the arched front entrance; the tall, narrow windows; and the lion downspouts all provided inspiration.

A view of the mansion's front door, decorated for the holidays.

Lions on the south and west side of the mansion double as waterspouts.

Special Techniques

Two-Tailed Two-Color Cast-On: Holding the MC over the index finger and the CC over the thumb, cast on the specified amount of stitches. The resulting stitches should be in MC.

Pattern Notes

After working the cuff, follow the chart.

The color work is done using the "stranded" method, carrying both colors at once. Avoid long floats on the inside on the mitten in those areas where more than five consecutive stitches are worked in one color by catching the color not in use with the working color.

Instructions

CUFF

With MC and CC, using two-tailed cast-on, CO 68 sts. PM at beg of rnd and join, taking care not to twist sts.

Rnd 1: *K1 MC, k1 CC; rep from * around.

Rnd 2: *Bring both yarns to the front, bring MC under CC and purl with MC; bring CC under MC strand, purl with CC; rep from * around. **Note**: This will twist every st and make the first row of the braid.

Rnd 3: *Leave both yarns to the front, bring MC, over CC and purl with MC, bring CC over MC strand, purl with CC; rep from * around. **Note**: This will make the second row of the braid, but with the twists leaning the opposite direction. It will also untwist all of the twisting that was created on Rnd 2.

Rnd 4: With MC knit, inc 10 sts evenly spaced around cuff—78 sts.

MAIN MITTEN

Rnds 1–30: Foll chart Rnds 1–30.

THUMB OPENING

Left Mitten—Rnd 31: Working Chart Rnd 31, work 19 sts, k20 sts with waste yarn, slip these sts back to the left needle, cont in pat.

Right Mitten—Rnd 31: Working Chart Rnd 31, k20 sts onto waste yarn, slip these sts back to left needle, cont in pat.

BOTH MITTENS

Cont to foll Chart A to Rnd 67.

RIGHT MITTEN DECREASES

Rnd 1: *K1 CC, k5 MC; rep from * around.

Rnd 2: *Ssk in CC, k4 MC; rep from * around—65 sts.

Rnds 3–4: *K1 CC, k4 MC; rep from * around.

Rnd 5: *Ssk in CC, k3 MC; rep from * around—52 sts.

Rnds 6–7: *K1 in CC, k3 in MC; rep from * around.

Rnd 8: *Ssk in CC, k2 MC; rep from * around—39 sts.

Rnd 9: *K1 in CC, k2 in MC; rep from * around.

Rnd 10: *Ssk in CC, k1 in MC; rep from * around—26 sts.

Rnd 11: *Ssk in CC; rep from * around—13 sts.

Break off yarn, leaving a 6"/15cm tail.

With tapestry needle, thread yarn through rem sts and pull tight; secure tails on WS.

LEFT MITTEN DECREASES
Rnd 1: *K1 CC, k5 MC; rep around.

Rnd 2: *K2tog in CC, k4 MC; rep from * around—65 sts.

Rnds 3–4: *K1 CC, k4 MC; rep from * around.

Rnd 5: *K2tog in CC, k3 MC, rep from * around—52 sts.

Rnds 6–7: *K1 in CC, k3 in MC; rep from * around.

Rnd 8: *K2tog in CC, k2 MC; rep from * around—39 sts.

Rnd 9: *K1 in CC, k2 in MC; rep from * around.

Rnd 10: *K2tog in CC, k1 in MC; rep from * around—26 sts.

Rnd 11: *K2tog in CC; rep from * around—13 sts.
Break off yarn, leaving a 6"/15cm tail.
With tapestry needle, thread yarn through rem sts and pull tight; secure tail on WS.

THUMB
Remove waste yarn and place the 20 sts onto needle, pm, pick up additional 20 sts around back of thumb opening—40 sts.
Foll Thumb Chart, working dec rnd every rnd three times as folls:

Decrease Rnd: K1, ssk, k to within 2 sts of next marker, k2tog, k 1, ssk, k to within last 2 sts ssk (4 sts dec'd).
Cont to work even foll Thumb Chart to Rnd 22.
Rep dec rnd every rnd six times—5 sts rem.
Break off yarn, leaving a 6"/15cm tail.
With tapestry needle, thread yarn through rem sts and pull tight; secure tail on WS.

FINISHING
Weave in all ends. Block.

Mansion Mittens Charts

THUMB CHART – LEFT THUMB

THUMB CHART – RIGHT THUMB

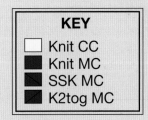

KEY	
☐	Knit CC
■	Knit MC
◣	SSK MC
◢	K2tog MC

CHAPTER 4

Traditional Knitting Techniques

People in costume at Rättvik, Sweden, 1914.
AMERICAN SWDEISH INSTITUTE COLLECTION

We don't think you can use the word "traditional" too much! Swedish mittens, Bohus-inspired, and twined knitting—traditional techniques unique to Sweden—are the focus of this chapter. Emma Jacobson is much revered for pioneering the Bohus Stickning cottage industry in Sweden. The Bohus-inspired items in this chapter draw a connection between Bohus knitting in Sweden during the 1940s and some of the art and architecture in the ASI. The twined knitting projects provide an introduction to the variety of twined techniques and the unique fabric that those techniques create.

Swedish Mittens
Two-Color Knitting

Size
Adult's Large

Finished Measurements
Circumference: 8 oz/20.5cm
Length: 10"/25.5cm

Materials

- Palette by Knitpicks, 100% Peruvian Highland wool, 50g/1.75oz, 231yds/211m:
- Currant (MC) and Sweet Potato (CC), 1 skein each
- Size 2 (2.75mm) double-pointed needles or size needed to obtain gauge
- Stitch markers
- Waste yarn (same size as mitten yarn or smaller)
- Tapestry needle

Gauge
32 sts and 33 rows = 4"/ 10 cm in St st.
Adjust needle size as necessary to obtain the correct gauge.

We've been fascinated by the small, repeating motifs of Swedish mittens for quite some time. With a copy of Ingrid Gottfridsson's *The Mitten Book* in hand, we each set off to study the motifs, plotting which mittens to make first and dreaming of designing our own someday. So when it came time to design our version of Swedish mittens for this book, this particular motif quickly came to mind. The "X O" pattern is a symbol of fertility that is most often worn by women. Inspiration for this motif came from cross-stitches that were embroidered on the cuff of a blouse in the ASI collection. This embellishment was thought to bring good luck to whomever wore the blouse.

The slanting cuff motif came from an old pattern by Joan Schrouder. Joan's pattern stated that a multiple of four for a 2x2 ribbing, plus one stitch, will make the ribbing slant to the left. Likewise, a 2x2 multiple ribbing, minus a stitch, will make the ribbing slant to the right. We added the extra color to add interest and make it unique.

The cross-stitched motif on the edge of this folk costume is said to be a fertility symbol commonly worn by women. This motif inspired the stitch design used in the Swedish Mittens.

AMERICAN SWEDISH INSTITUTE COLLECTION

Instructions

RIGHT MITTEN

Cuff

With MC and dpns, CO 49 sts. Pm at beg of rnd. Divide sts evenly on dpns and join, taking care not to twist sts.
Knit 8 rnds.
Left-slanting ribbing: *With CC p2; with MC k2; rep from * for 24 rnds.
Note: On all future rnds you will see that the ribbing jogs 1 st to the left.
With MC k 1 rnd, inc 11 sts evenly around—60 sts.
Purl 1 rnd.

Hand

Rnds 1–14: Work Chart A Rnds 1–14, reading chart from right to left.
Rnd 15: Work to red line for right thumb opening. Using waste yarn, k11 sts, transfer these 11 sts back to left needle, and cont to foll chart. Cont to foll chart to tip of mitten, working dec rnds on chart as foll: K2tog, cont chart to last 2 sts, ssk.

Thumb

Carefully pull out waste yarn, placing sts on two dpns.
Note: You will have 11 sts on front needle and 11 sts on back needle. Foll Thumb Chart, working dec rnds on chart in same manner as for hand.

LEFT MITTEN

Cuff

With MC and dpns, CO 47 sts. Pm at beg of rnd. Divide sts evenly on dpns and join, taking care not to twist sts.
Knit 8 rnds.
Right-slanting ribbing: *With CC p2; with MC k2; rep from * for 24 rnds. **Note**: On all future rnds you will see that the ribbing jogs 1 st to the right.
With MC, k 1 rnd, inc 13 sts evenly around—60 sts.
Purl 1 rnd.

Hand

Rnds 1–14: Work Chart A Rnds 1–14, reading chart from right to left.
Rnd 15: Work to red line for left thumb opening. Using waste yarn, k11 sts; transfer these 11 sts back to left needle and cont to foll chart.
Cont to foll chart to tip of mitten working dec rnds on chart as foll: K2tog, cont chart to last 2 sts, ssk.

Thumb

Carefully pull out waste yarn, placing sts on 2 dpns. **Note**: You will have 11 sts on front needle and 11 sts on back needle. Foll Thumb Chart working dec rnds on chart in same manner as for hand.

FINISHING
Weave in all ends. Block.

CHART A

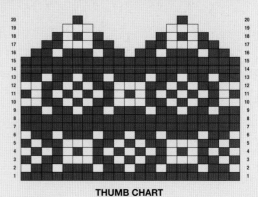

THUMB CHART

Twined-Knit Christmas Sock

Finished Measurements

Circumference at top of stocking: 14"/35.5cm
Length from top of stocking to bottom of heel: 15"/38cm

Materials

- Knit Picks Gloss DK, 70% merino/30% silk, 50g/1.75oz. 123yds/112m: Cream #24985 (MC), 4 skeins Scarlet #24987 (CC) OR Jade #24728 (CC), 2 skeins
- Off-white #263 (MC), 3 skeins
- Red #969 (CC), 1 skein
- Size 5 (mm) double-pointed needles (set of 5) and 16"/40.5cm long circular needle or size needle to obtain gauge
- Stitch markers (one in CC for beg of rnd)
- Tapestry needle

Gauge

20 sts and 20 rnds = 4"/10cm in twined knitting technique. *Adjust needle size as necessary to obtain correct gauge.*

This sock design is intended to be a sampler of the twined knitting techniques. The pattern provides step-by-step instruction, covering various techniques in each section of the sock, making this project a great choice for anyone new to twined knitting. Twined knitting is sometimes called "two-ended" knitting, because it is most often done with two strands of the same color yarn, pulled from the same yarn ball. In this pattern, though, we started the sock using two colors to make it easier for the beginner to see how the twining is done.

The goat motif featured on this sock is drawn from one of the oldest Scandinavian Christmas symbols, the Yule Goat. Before the nineteenth century, Scandinavians believed that the goat provided the presents during the holidays. Even though the *Jultomte* (Father Christmas) later replaced the goat, many Swedish families still maintain the tradition of having a straw goat in the house for the holidays.

(CONTINUED ON PAGE 92)

Twined Cast-On

STEP 1: With two ends of the MC ball and one strand of the CC ball, make an overhand knot on needle. Note that this knot is not part of the stitch count and will be removed when joining round.

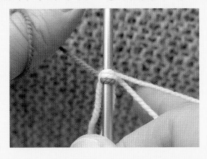

STEP 2: Starting with the two MC stands in the right hand and the CC stand over the left hand thumb.

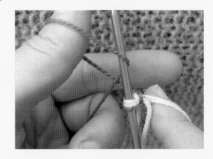

STEP 3: Insert needle into left-hand thumb loop of CC.

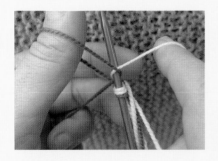

STEP 4: Bring back right hand MC strand over the tip of needle to make stitch over needle.

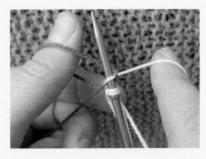

STEP 5: Draw CC up and over needle tip so that yarn wraps around MC stitch.

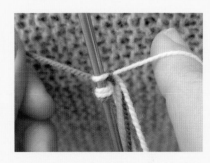

STEP 6: Pull CC snug to hold stitch on needle. Then return to starting position.

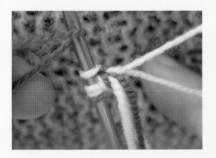

STEP 7: Insert needle into left thumb loop of CC, and with second strand of MC lifted over first strand (from first CO sts), wrap over MC over needle.

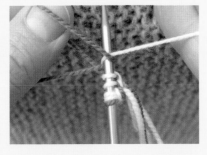

STEP 8: Continue to CO using the alternating MC strands, always remember to bring the strand over the previous strand (twining or twisting) them over one another as you form the CP stitches.

STEP 9: Shows the final CO result. Alternating strands of MC and the MC strand making a nice accent edge on the CO.

Twined Knitting

STEP 1: Hold both strands in back of work, separating the strands with index finger.

STEP 2: Carry MC stand over the CC and knit with MC.

STEP 3: Bring CC under CC and forward.

STEP 4: Knit with CC.

STEP 5: Final appearance of twined knitting.

Bottom Right: Back side of twined knitting.

STEP 1

STEP 2

STEP 3

STEP 4

STEP 5

Twined Purling

STEP 1: Hold both strands in the front of the work.

STEP 2: Bring MC under CC and purl with MC.

STEP 3: Bring CC under CC strand.

STEP 4: Purl with CC.

STEP 5: Resulting twist from purling and twisting every other color.

STEP 1

STEP 2

STEP 3

STEP 4

STEP 5

Twined Knitting Technique

From the province of Darlana, Sweden, comes the very unusual style of knitting called *tvåändssticking*, which means "two-ends knitting." This technique is often called two-ended knitting or twined knitting because between each stitch, the two yarn strands (both coming from the same ball) are twisted around each other. The resulting fabric is extremely durable and almost windproof. The reverse side of the twined knitted fabric looks much like the older needle looping technique of *nålbindning*.

The technique of twined knitting is better suited for the knitter who "throws" and carries the yarn in the right hand. Some historical research has shown that once English knitting, or "picking" with yarn in the left hand, was introduced in Swedish public schools, two-ended knitting started to fade.

The ball of yarn used for twined knitting must be wound so that both ends of the ball can be used at the same time. Some yarns that are not spun tightly tend to unspin with the constant twisting of the strands. Swedish knitters use a special Z-spun yarn, but any firmly spun yarn will work.

One frustration you may encounter when using the twined knitting technique is the continual twisting of the yarn ends, which causes the two strands of yarn to become twisted. To combat the twisting, a few methods have been used successfully. Any of these methods will work, depending on your knitting location.

- First, use a spare double-pointed needle to secure the strands to the ball, so that no extra yarn is unwound from the ball. Let the ball hang suspended and it will untwist. This is similar to using a knitting hook.
- The second method, which can only be done when there is plenty of elbow room, is to stab the ball of yarn with a spare needles and spin the ball around the needles in the direction that untwists the strands. This method is a bit more dangerous, but effective, until the ball of yarn goes flying across the room.
- The third method is to use a yarn lazy Susan, a fairly new invention made with two circles of wood, ball bearings, and a dowel. Stick the ball of yarn onto the dowel and spin the ball around to untwist the yarn.

For more information on the twined knitting technique, see the Twined Knitting entries in the bibliography.

Crook Stitches

Worked with one strand in front used to purl and the other strand in the back used to knit. This is the only twined knitting technique in which the yarns are not twisted on each stitch.

STEP 1: Bring one strand to the front of work.

STEP 2: Purl next st with front strand of yarn. Leave strand in front of work.

STEP 3: Knit the next st with the back strand of yarn, Leave strand in back of work.

STEP 4: Oftentimes the crook sts are used to form a chain path by working a second round of crook sts, which is offset by one stitch.

STEP 1

STEP 2

STEP 3

STEP 4

Deep Stitches

STEP 1: Bring both yarns to the front of work.

STEP 2: Purl with both yarns held together.

STEP 3: Bring yarns to back of work.

STEP 1

STEP 2

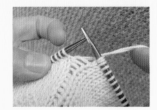

STEP 3

Single Purl Stitch

STEP 1: Bring single strand of yarn to front of work.

STEP 2: Purl with single strand of yarn.

STEP 3: Bring yarn to back of work.

STEP 1

STEP 2

STEP 3

STEP 1-A

STEP 1-B

STEP 2

STEP 3

STEP 4

STEP 5

After-Thought Stitch Pick-Up

Notice that the sts from the waste yarn are really loops that are actually between the sts. To remedy this, the first row of "loop-sts" are worked in the following manner. Continuing in twined knitting with MC, attach two ends of the yarn.

STEP 1: Stick right needle into the back of two loops.

STEP 2: Wrap yarn around as if knitting two sts together.

STEP 3: Continue knitting motion by pulling loop through both sts.

STEP 4: Slip off only the first loop, keeping the second loop on the left needle.

STEP 5: Stick the right needle into the back of the remaining loop and the next loop on left needle. Continue until all the loops are worked.

(CONTINUED FROM PAGE 86)

Special Techniques

Twined Knitting (see Special Techniques Used, page 140)

Pattern Notes

The sock begins with a traditional three-strand cast-on used in twined knitting. It is easier to cast the sts onto one straight needle and then move to the circular needle.

The basic techniques in the sock are
- Three-strand cast-on
- Two-color twined knitting
- Two-color twined purling
- One-color twined knitting
- Crook stitches
- Three-strand, two-color pattern knitting (in a goat or tree pattern)
- Use of "deep" stitches to make a false seam, or "part", down the back of the sock
- Single Purl Stitch for Clock pattern
- Special stitch pick-up technique for the afterthought foot and toe

Instructions

With two strands of MC and one strand of CC using twined CO method, CO 108 sts. Pm for beg of rnd and join, taking care not to twist sts.

CUFF

Foll Chart A as foll:

Rnd 1: Work one rnd of two-color twined knitting with one strand of MC and one strand of CC (this is the set-up row for the twined purling—braid). **Note**: Without this set-up row, the braid will not work out as nicely.

Rnd 2: Work one rnd of twined purling in two colors.

Rnds 3–11: Work two-color twined knitting for nine rows.

Rnd 12: Work 1 rnd of twined purling in two colors as before; do not break off CC but attach second end of MC.

Rnd 13: Work 1 rnd of twined knitting with two ends of the MC ball.

Rnd 14: Work 1 rnd of crook sts.

Rnds 15–16: Work 2 rnds of twined knitting with MC.

YULE GOAT OR TREE PATTERN

Attach one strand of CC and foll Chart A for Goat or Tree pat. Maintain two strands for the MC. Be sure to continue to twist the yarns after each st to maintain a consistent tension throughout the sock. This is not normal two-color stranded knitting because of the twisting strands on each st. **Note**: When the three yarns get twisted, take time to untwist the balls. If the third strand causes too much tangling, then break off a length of CC to complete work.

After completing Goat or Tree Chart, work 2 rnds of twined knitting in MC.

SOCK BODY

Rnd 1: Work 1 rnd of crook sts with MC.

Rnd 2: Work 1 rnd of twined knitting with MC.

Rnd 3: Work set-up rnd of two-color twined knitting with MC and CC.

Rnd 4: Work 1 rnd of twined purling in the two colors; break off CC.

Rnd 5: Work 1 rnd of twined knitting.

Note: From now until the heel, the first st of the rnd will be a "deep" st. Bring both MC yarns forward and p1; bring yarns to back, twin knit rem sts.

Work Chart B while maintaining the first st of rnd in the "deep" st pat, which will create a false seam down the back of the sock—this is a very traditional element in a twined knit sock.

SOCK DECREASES

Rnds 1–7: P1 (deep st), k to end.

Rnd 8: P1 (deep st), k1, k2tog, work until 3 sts from end of rnd, ssk, k1—106 sts.

Rep dec Rnds 1–8 two more times—102 sts.

CLOCK PATTERN

Rnd 1: P1 (deep st), k20, pm, work Chart C over next 13 sts, pm, k35, pm, work Chart C over next 13 sts; on back side k20 to end of rnd. Cont as est working Chart C on each side of sock; at the same time cont to dec every 8th rnd, maintaining deep sts as est. Work until Chart C is complete—96 sts rem. Work 2 rnds of twined knitting without the deep st in the center back.

Note: The traditional construction method for a twined sock is to knit a waste yarn in, but in the position for an "after-thought foot/toe," not the normal "after-thought heel." The idea is that if the heel is worked before the foot and toe, the sock can be tried on to measure the length of the sock against the person's foot. This is not possible with the typical after-thought heel, because the sock cannot be tried on until the heel is completed and if this is the last step, the length of the foot and toe have already been determined. Very clever, those Swedes of Dalarna!

HEEL SET-UP

Rnd 1: K24 with CC, then k48 with waste yarn (in foot and toe position), slip waste yarn sts back to left needle, and k24 with CC to end. Pm after the 24th and 72nd sts in the rnd to mark dec areas.

HEEL

With CC, k to 3 sts from marker, ssk, k1, slm (slip marker), k1, k2tog, k to 3 sts from marker ssk, k1, slm, k1, k2tog, k to end. Cont to dec every other rnd until 24 sts rem. Lay the needles parallel and Kitchener stitch together.

AFTER-THOUGHT FOOT AND TOE

Place the sts that were placed on "hold" onto a needle. Remove the waste yarn holding the other half of the sts. Use the After-Thought Stitch Pick-up shown on page 91. Cont in twined knitting with MC, attach two ends of the yarn, insert right needle into the back of two loops, knit and slip off only the first loop, keeping the second one on the left needle. Next insert the right needle into the back of the rem loop and the next loop on the left needle; k, slipping off only the first loop, cont until all the loops are worked.

If necessary, pick up and k2 sts in the heel corner to avoid holes, twined knit around the held sts, then pick up and k2 sts in the other heel corner. Work twined knit for 40 rnds. Break off MC and attach CC. Work toe decs in the same manner as the heel.

FINISHING

Weave in all ends.

Make braid using the long tails from the cast-on, fold over, and secure to cuff to make loop for hanging. Block and wait for the Christmas Goat to bring you lots of presents!

TREE CHART

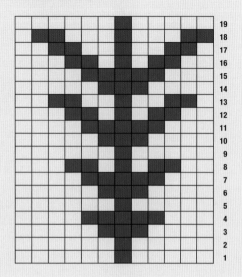

RIBBING GOAT CHART

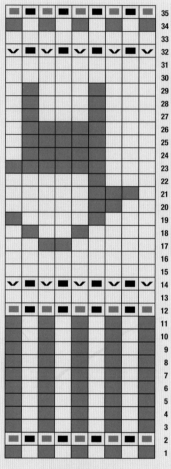

CHART A

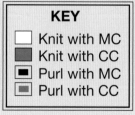

KEY

☐	Knit with MC
▨	Knit with CC
▣	Purl with MC
▨	Purl with CC

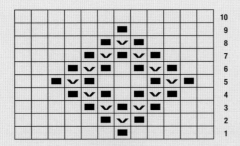

CHART B

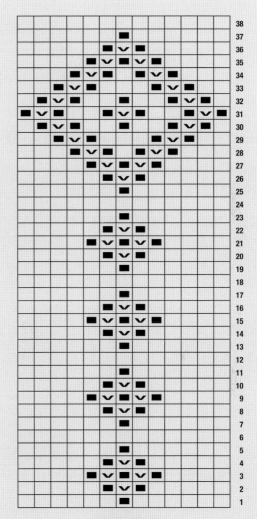

CHART C

Twined-Knit Fingerless Gloves

Size
Adult's Average

Finished Measurements
Circumference: 7"/18cm
Length: 5"/12.5cm

Materials

- Knit Picks Gloss DK, 70% merino/30% silk, 50g/1.75oz. 123yds/112m: Coast Grey #24724 (MC) and Cranberry #24725 (CC), 1 skein each OR Cream #24985 (MC) and Celestial #25588 (CC), 1 skein each
- Grey #221 (MC) and Red #969 (CC), 1 skein each
- Size 4 (3.5mm) double-pointed needles (set of 5) and 16"/40.5cm long circular needle or size needle to obtain gauge
- Waste yarn
- Stitch markers (one in CC for beg of rnd)
- Stitch holders
- Tapestry needle

Gauge
20 sts and 20 rnds = 4"/10cm in twined knitting technique. *Adjust needle size as necessary to obtain correct gauge.*

This pattern for a twined fingerless glove uses the two-color twined method with crook stitches to create a mosaic-type pattern on the cuff. The two-color stripe pattern is carried throughout the glove, but the second color is not apparent in the area where the crook stitches are worked. This is because here the stripes appear to be horizontal, fooling the eye into thinking there is only one color in each row, which is not the case.

In traditional Swedish knitting, often items were knit with natural colors of the wool, such as black and white. The garment was then dyed red to achieve a uniform background color. At the Nordiska Museet in Stockholm, we saw examples of woven wool jackets with twined knit sleeves in black and red. Although there are no examples of this knitting style in the ASI collection, we felt it was an important characteristic of Swedish knitting and chose to include this set of black-and-red fingerless gloves as a reminder of the past practice.

Special Techniques

Twined Knitting (see Special Techniques Used, page 140)

Long-Tailed Cast-On (see Special Techniques Used, page 140)

Instructions

With one strand each of MC and CC, using the twined cast-on method (See Step-by-Step Twined Knitting photos), CO 54 sts. Pm for beg of rnd and join, taking care not to twist sts.

CUFF (SAME FOR LEFT AND RIGHT HANDS)

Foll Chart A, work as foll:

Rnds 1 and 3: Work 1 rnd of two-color crook sts, holding CC in the front of work and MC in the back.

Rnd 2: Work 1 rnd of two-color crook sts, holding MC in the front of work and CC in the back.

Rnds 4–10: Cont to work two-color crook sts, but begin the diamond pat by bringing the front yarn to the back and k that st as indicated on chart.

Rnds 11–14: Rep Rnds 1–3, then Rnd 2 to complete cuff.

LEFT HAND

Rnd 15: Work two-color twined knit as est, pm in the 25th st (CC) to mark center thumb gusset st.

Rnd 16: Work to marked st, M1 in CC, k1 CC, M1 in CC, work to end—56 sts.

Rnd 17: Work to marked st, M1 in MC, k1 CC, M1 in MC, work to end—58 sts.

Rnd 18: Work two-color twined knit as est.

Rnd 19: Rep Rnd 16—60 sts.

Rnd 20: Rep Rnd 17—62 sts.

Rnd 21: Work 38 sts, pm, work Chart B, pm, work to end.

Rnds 22–31: Cont to inc as est while working Chart B in the center top of hand—74 sts at end of Rnd 31.

Rnds 32–35: Work 4 rnds with no incs, cont to work Chart B.

Rnd 36: Work 23 sts, place next 23 sts on a holder, CO 3 sts, matching the two-color pat, join to other side of thumb hole, work to end.

Rnds 37–44: Work as est, work in two-color twined knit after completing Chart B.

RIGHT HAND

Rnd 15: Work two-color twined knit as est, pm in the 31th st (CC) to mark center thumb gusset st.

Rnd 16: Work to marked st, M1 in CC, k1 CC, M1

in CC, work to end—56 sts.

Rnd 17: Work to marked st, M1 in MC, k1 CC, M1 in MC, work to end—58 sts.

Rnd 18: Work two-color twined knit as est.

Rnd 19: Rep Rnd 16—60 sts.

Rnd 20: Rep Rnd 17—62 sts.

Rnd 21: Work 6 sts, pm, work Chart B, pm, work to end.

Rnds 22–31: Cont to inc as est while working Chart B in the center top of hand—74 sts at end of Rnd 31.

Rnd 32–35: Work 4 rnds with no incs, cont to work Chart B.

Rnd 36: Work 29 sts, place next 23 sts on a holder, CO 3 sts, matching the two-color pat, join to other side of thumb hole, work to end.

Rnds 37–44: Work as est, work in two-color twined knit after completing Chart B.

TOP EDGE (FOR LEFT AND RIGHT GLOVES)

Rnds 45–48: Rep Rnds 1–2 twice, BO in two-color twined knit with CC in front and MC in back of work. Secure ends.

THUMB

Remove waste yarn and place 23 sts on dpns; pick up 5 sts (3 from CO and 1 in each corner) along inside of thumb, matching the color pat—28 sts.

Work two-color twined knit for 6 rnds. Work 4 rnds of top edge pat to finish.

FINISHING

Weave in all ends. Block.

Celestial/cream colorway, Knit Picks Gloss dk merino/ silk blend, colors celestial and cream.

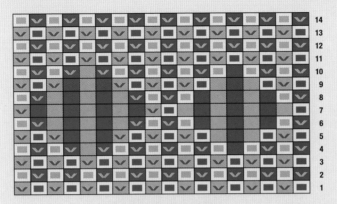

CHART A—CUFF

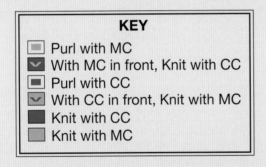

KEY

- Purl with MC
- With MC in front, Knit with CC
- Purl with CC
- With CC in front, Knit with MC
- Knit with CC
- Knit with MC

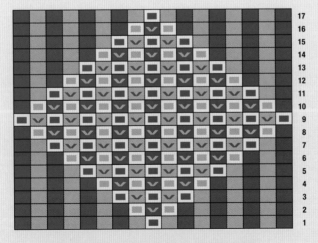

CHART B—DIAMOND PATTERN

Sidna's Sweater

The diamond motif used in Sidna's sweater was inspired by a red and white cross-stitched cloth from the Swedish home of Eric Orlow's mother. A family friend donated the beautiful cloth to the ASI in 1998.

Special Techniques
Three-Needle Bind-Off (see Special Techniques Used, page 140)

Pattern Notes
Although circular needles are recommended for knitting this sweater, it is not knit in the round but rather back and forth in one piece. At the armholes the stitches are divided for left front, back, and right front. Each of these sections is then worked separately, back and forth.

Instructions

BODY
With smaller needles, CO 183 (203, 223, 243) sts. *Do not join.*Work K1, p1 ribbing for 2"/5cm, ending after a WS row.

CROOK STITCHES
Row 1: *P1, wyif sl 1; rep from * across.
Row 2 and all even rows: Purl.
Row 3: *Sl 1 wyif, p1; rep from * across.
Row 4: Purl.

Sizes
Woman's Small (Medium, Large, X-Large)

Finished Measurements
Chest: 36 ½ (40 ½, 44, 48)"/92.5 (103, 112, 122)cm
Length: 25 (25 ½, 26, 26 ½)"/63.5 (65, 66, 67.5)cm

Materials

- Brown Sheep Company's Nature Spun, 100% wool, 100g/3.5oz, 245yds/224m:
- Blue Boy #116, 6 (6, 7, 7) skeins.
- Sizes 5 (3.75mm) and 7 (4.5mm) double-pointed needles and 24"/61cm long circular needles or size needed to obtain gauge
- Buttons (10)
- Stitch holders
- Tapestry needle

Gauge
20 sts and 28 rows = 4"/10cm in St st on larger needles. *Adjust needle size as necessary to obtain correct gauge.*

This red and white cross-stitched cloth from the Swedish home of Eric Orlow's mother inspired the stitch patterns in Sidna's Sweater. A family friend donated the beautiful cloth to ASI in 1998.
AMERICAN SWEDISH INSTITUTE COLLECTION

BORDER PATTERN

K0 (4, 2, 0) sts, follow Chart A working first st, then work 12-st rep 15 (16, 18, 20) times, working last 2 sts on chart, then k0 (4, 2, 0) sts. Cont as est until Chart A has been completed.

Work in St st until piece measures 15 (15 ½, 16, 16 ½)"/38 (39.5, 40.5, 42) cm from beg, ending after a WS row.

DIVIDE FOR ARMHOLES

Next Row (RS): Place 42 (47, 52, 57) sts on holder for left front, place next 8 sts on separate holder for underarm, leave next 83 (93, 103, 113) sts on needle for back, place next 8 sts on separate holder for underarm, place last 42 (47, 52, 57) sts on holder for right front.

BACK DIAMOND CHEVRON

Next Row (RS): K7 (12, 17, 22) sts, then work Chart B over the next 69 sts, k7 (12, 17, 22) sts.
Cont as est until Chart B has been completed.
Work four rows of St st.
Rep Rows 1–4 of crook sts.
Work two rows St st.
Rep Rows 1–4 of crook sts.
Work four rows St st.
Place 23 (28, 33, 36) sts on holder for shoulder, 37 sts on holder for back neck, then 23 (28, 33, 36) sts for other shoulder.

RIGHT FRONT

Place 42 (47, 52, 57) sts from right front holder onto larger needle.
Next Row (RS): Beg with center st on Chart B, work right half of chart on 35 sts, then k7 (12, 17, 22) sts to end to row. Cont as est until Chart B has been completed.
On next row, place 9 sts at neck edge on holder, then work in St st for four rows, dec 1 st at neck edge every row.
Rep Rows 1–4 of crooks sts and cont to dec 1 st on neck edge every row.
Work two rows in St st and cont to dec 1 st at neck edge every row.
Rep Rows 1–4 of crook sts without neck edge decs.
Work four rows in St st.
Use three-needle bind-off to join 23 (28, 33, 38) sts to back shoulder sts.

LEFT FRONT

Remove 42 (47, 52, 57) sts from holder and place on needle.
Next Row (RS): K7 (12, 17, 22) sts beg with center st on Chart B, work left half of chart on 35 sts. Cont as est until Chart B has been completed.
On next row, place 9 sts at neck edge on holder, then work in St st for four rows, dec 1 st at neck edge every row.
Rep Rows 1–4 of crook sts and cont to dec 1 st at neck edge every row.
Work two rows in St st and cont to dec 1 st at neck edge every row.
Rep Rows 1–4 of crook sts without neck edge decs.
Use three-needle bind-off to join 23 (28, 33, 38) sts to back shoulder sts.

SLEEVES

With RS facing and larger circular needle, pick up and k100 sts around armhole, then place 8 sts from underarm holder onto needle—108 sts. The first eight rows are worked back and forth, joining sleeve to underarm with an ssk at the beg of row as foll:

Rows 1–4: Work Rows 1–4 of crook sts.

Rows 5–6: Work in St st.

Rows 7–8: Work Rows 1–2 of crook sts.

Once all the underarm sts have been attached, join and beg working in-the-rnd.

Dec Rnd: K1, ssk, knit to last 2 sts, k2tog.

Rep dec rnd every 5th rnd, at the same time working 39 rnds of Chart C in the center 31 sts of the sleeve. Cont until sleeve meas 6"/15cm less than desired length.

Work 21 rds of Chart D in the center of the sleeve.

Work 2 rnds in St st.

Work 4 rows of crook st, working back and forth.

Change to smaller dpns and work k1, p1 rib for 3"/7.5cm. BO in rib.

NECK

With RS facing and smaller circular needle, pick up and k24 sts along right front edge of neck; k back sts from holder onto needle, then pick up and k24 sts along left front neck edge.

Working back and forth, work one row of crook sts, then work seven rows of k1, p1 rib. BO in rib.

BUTTON BAND

With RS facing and smaller circular needle, pick up and k130 (134, 138, 142) sts along left front opening. Work in k1, p1 rib for four rows. BO in rib. Mark for ten buttons evenly spaced on button band.

BUTTONHOLE BAND

With RS facing and smaller circular needle, pick up and k130 (134, 138, 142) sts along right front opening. Work in k1, p1 rib for two rows.

Buttonhole Row: Work in rib to next buttonhole marker, yf, slip 1 purlwise, yb, drop yarn, **slip next st and psso to dec 1, rep from * until desired number of buttonhole sts around bound-off, slip last st back to left-hand needle, turn work, yb, cable CO same number of sts bound off, plus one more. Turn work, slip 1 st, and pass extra CO st over slipped st; rep from ** across all buttonhole markers, rib to end of row.

Work 1 row in rib. BO in rib.

FINISHING

Sew buttons opposite buttonholes.

Weave in all ends. Block.

Sidna's Knitting: Faux Twined Knitting
(or Two-Ended Minus One)

We consider ourselves lucky to have known Sidna Farley as both a teacher and a friend. We first met Sidna at a weekend knitting retreat in Minneapolis, Minnesota, called Knitter's Days, where she was the guest teacher from Denver, Colorado.

We immediately fell in love with Sidna's relaxed and friendly teaching style. Over the years, every time she traveled through the Twin Cities on her way to Elizabeth Zimmerman's Oft-Timer's camp in Wisconsin, a group of knitters would get together with Sidna and her traveling companions for dinner and a "show and share" of wonderful techniques and projects. Many times, these latest designs would appear on the pages of popular knitting magazines over the next year.

Sidna was an innovative knitter who was always improving or modifying techniques. Her "two-ended minus one" technique was actually a mistaken interpretation of the Swedish twined knitting technique. She did not set out to invent a new method, rather she was trying to teach herself how to get the look of twined knitting. Instead of using the two strands of yarn and twisting one yarn over the other in alternating stitches, she achieved a similar look without all the weight of the actual twined knitting. She would slip the stitch with the yarn in front to get the look of the twined-knit "crook stitch" without having to use two yarns.

When Sidna died from Parkinson's Disease in 2007, it was a great loss to the knitting community. She touched many hands, including ours, and inspired them to create more. We thank Sidna for encouraging us to continue in knitting design.

SIDNA'S SWEATER DIAGRAM

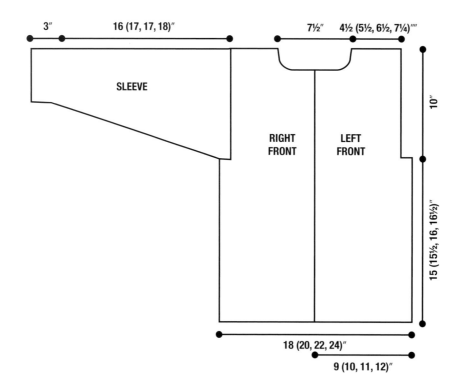

Sidna's Sweater Charts

SIDNA'S SLEEVE CHART C

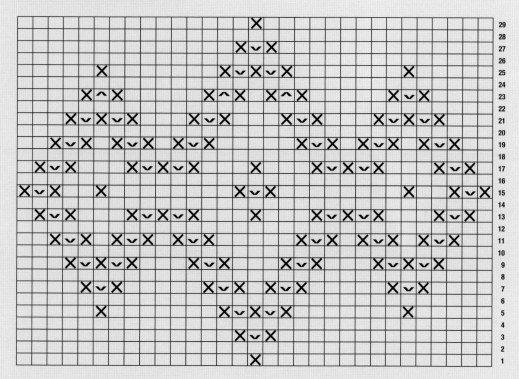

SIDNA'S SLEEVE CHART D

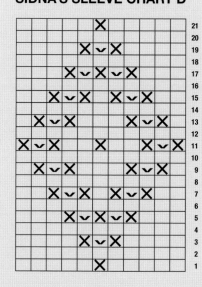

SIDNA'S BORDER CHART A

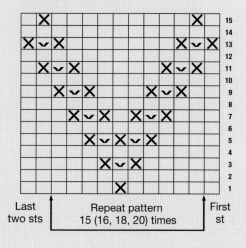

Last two sts
Repeat pattern 15 (16, 18, 20) times
First st

KEY
- ☐ Knit Stockinette
- ☒ Purl
- ☒⌣☒ Purl, with yarn forward, slip 1, Purl

SIDNA'S SWEATER CHART B

KEY

□	Knit Stockinette
✕	Purl
✕⟩✕	Purl, with yarn forward, slip 1, Purl

Bohus-Inspired Dressing Room Cowl

Look up during a tour of the American Swedish Institue and you'll notice that the elaborately detailed ceiling moldings are painted to match the porcelain stoves in many of the mansion's rooms. It was the crown molding in the dressing room that inspired this colorful and cozy cowl. The periwinkle color is the most striking shade in this design and the trick of finding just the right shade of yarn seemed the biggest hurdle. Classic Elite's Fresco, which has a percentage of the traditional Bohus fiber of angora, was the perfect choice. In the spirit of traditional Bohus knitting, this cowl features many colors in slight gradations, allowing the shades to blend perfectly and making the purl stitches "pop" as they are supposed to.

Special Techniques
Provisional Cast-On (see Special Techniques Used, page 140)
Kitchener Stitch (see Special Techniques Used, page 140)

Note: For a closer-fitting cowl, cast on a multiple of 10 sts less and foll instructions as written.

Finished Measurements
Circumference: 42"/106.5cm
Height: 8"/20.5cm

Materials

- Classic Elite Fresco, 60%wool/30% baby alpaca, 50g/1.75oz, 164yds/150m:
- Saxony Blue #5348 (MC), Parchment #5301 (A), Sweet Lilac #5354 (B), Sugar Blue #5304 (C), Corn Silk #5343 (D), Bittersweet #5318 (E), Ginger #5350 (F), Cornflower #5393 (G), Purple Haze #5379 (H), Magenta #5326 (I), Pansy #5356 (J), Max Factor Pink #5371 (K), 1 skein each
- Size 5 (3.75mm), 16"/40.5cm long circular needle or size needed to obtain gauge
- Size 4 (3.5mm), 16"/40.5cm long circular needles or one size smaller than size needed to obtain gauge (2)
- Waste yarn
- Stitch markers (one in CC for beg of rnd)
- Tapestry needle

Optional:
- Fleece for lining cowl
- Sewing thread to match fleece
- Straight pins

Gauge
24 sts and 24 rows = 4"/10cm in St st.
Adjust needle size as necessary to obtain correct gauge.

Bohus-Inspired
Dressing Room Cowl Chart

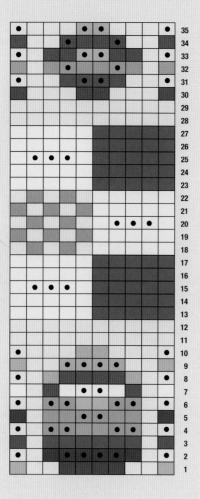

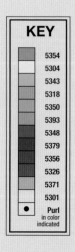

Instructions

STARTING HEM
Using provisional method and smaller circular needle, CO 240 sts. Pm for beg of rnd and join, being careful not to twist sts. With MC, knit 10 rnds.

Turning Rnd: *Yo, k2tog; rep from * to end of rnd. Knit 10 rnds.

Unzip provisional CO, placing live sts on second smaller needle; fold hem at turning rnd so that needles are parallel.

Joining Rnd: Using larger circular needle, *insert right tip into first st on front needle, then into first st on back needle and knit them tog; rep from * around—240 sts.

BODY
Rnds 1–4: With A, k.

Rnds 5–39: Foll chart, changing colors and incorporating purl sts as indicated.

Rnds 40–43: With A, k.

ENDING HEM
With MC, knit 5 rnds.

Turning Rnd: *Yo, k2tog; rep from * to end of rnd. Knit 5 rnds.

Using smaller circular needle, pick up 240 sts on inside of cowl. Using Kitchener stitch, close ending hem to picked-up sts.

FINISHING
Weave in all ends. Block.

LINING (OPTIONAL)
Using finished cowl as guide, measure and cut the lining with the width slightly wider and the length 1"/2.5cm longer than the cowl. Sew seam using ½"/1.25cm seam allowance. Pin lining in place on WS of the cowl at the hem of each picot edge. Using a whipstitch, hand sew lining in place.

The ceiling details in the Dressing Room were the inspiration for the Dressing Room Cowl.
AMERICAN SWEDISH INSTITUTE COLLECTION

Examples of the beautiful color work on Bohus sweaters.
AMERICAN SWEDISH INSTITUTE COLLECTION

Bohus-Inspired Birch Tree Hat

This birch tree hat offers a new twist on the Bohus tradition. Bohus knitting is often thought of as a rhythmic repeat of short patterns, using purl stitches to blend many similar hues and create a gradation of color. It is less known that in the early years of the Bohus cooperative, embroidery was also used on a number of the plain mitten designs to enhance the texture and add decoration. Both purl stitches and embroidery are used in this hat to achieve a unique reflection of the birch tree.

Special Techniques
Provisional Cast-On (see Special Techniques Used, page 140).
Kitchener Stitch (see Special Techniques Used, page 140)

Size
Adult's Average

Finished Measurements
Head circumference:
20"/51cm
Length: 9"/23cm

Materials

- Cascade 220, 100% wool, 100g/3.5oz, 220yds/201m:
- *Rust Version*: Forest Green Heather #9486 (MC), White #8505 (A), Black #8555 (B), Rust #9460 (C), Green Heather #3176 (D), 1 skein each
- *Green Version*: Forest Green Heather #9486 (MC), White #8505 (A), Black #8555 (B), Lt. Green Heather #3176 (C), Green Heather #9460 (D), 1 skein each
- Size 7 (4.5mm) double-pointed (set of 5) and 16"/40.5cm long circular needles or size needed to obtain gauge
- Size 6 (4 mm) 16"/40.5cm long circular needle
- Waste yarn
- Stitch markers, two in CC (for beg of rnd and center stitch)
- Tapestry needle

Gauge
20 sts and 20 rnds = 4"/10cm in stranded two-color St st on larger needles.
Adjust needle size as necessary to obtain correct gauge.

This oil painting, made by Axel Julius Gabriel Lindahl in 1932, inspired the Birch Hat. Lindahl was trained as a painter of theatrical backdrops, and the overall decorative quality of the painting gave us the idea to use the birch theme in a knitted item.
AMERICAN SWEDISH INSTITUTE COLLECTION

Pattern Notes

Hat is worked in the round; change to dpns when stitches no longer fit comfortably on circular needle.

The facing is worked on a smaller needle to get a tighter fit; after brim pattern is complete, the facing is folded inside hat and fused to brim using a three-needle join technique.

Instructions

FACING

With smaller needle and MC, and waste yarn, use crochet CO method, CO 112 sts. Pm for beg of rnd and join, taking care not to twist sts.
Knit 20 rnds.
Next Rnd (turning ridge): Purl.

CUFF

Change to larger needle.
Knit 1 rnd.
Attach C and work Chart A.
Attach D and work Chart B. Break off C and D.

Next Rnd (three-needle join): Remove CO sts from waste yarn and place them on smaller needle. Fold facing inside cuff so that WSs are tog. (The larger needle with cuff sts should be on the outside and the smaller needle with the facing sts should be lined up on the inside of the hat.) Holding needles parallel and using MC, *knit tog 1 st from the front needle and 1 from the back needle; rep from * around until all sts are joined.
Next Rnd: With MC, purl and dec 4 sts evenly spaced on the last rnd—108 sts. Pm after 54th st to mark center.

MAIN HAT

Rnds 1–30: Work 30 rnds foll Bohus Birch Chart C.
Rnd 31 (dec): Maintaining the charted pat throughout decreasing, *k1, ssk, k to within 2 sts from m, k2tog; rep from * around—104 sts.
Rnds 32–41 (dec): Cont to work charted pat, rep dec rnd every rnd.
Rnd 42: Knit.
Break yarn, leaving a 12"/30.5cm tail.
Fold rem sts in half and join using Kitchener stitch; secure end on WS.

FINISHING

Embroidery: With C, chainstitch an outline around each leaf motif on the hat band. Backstitch once for leaf stem.
Weave in all ends. Block.

Bohus-Inspired Birch Tree Hat Charts

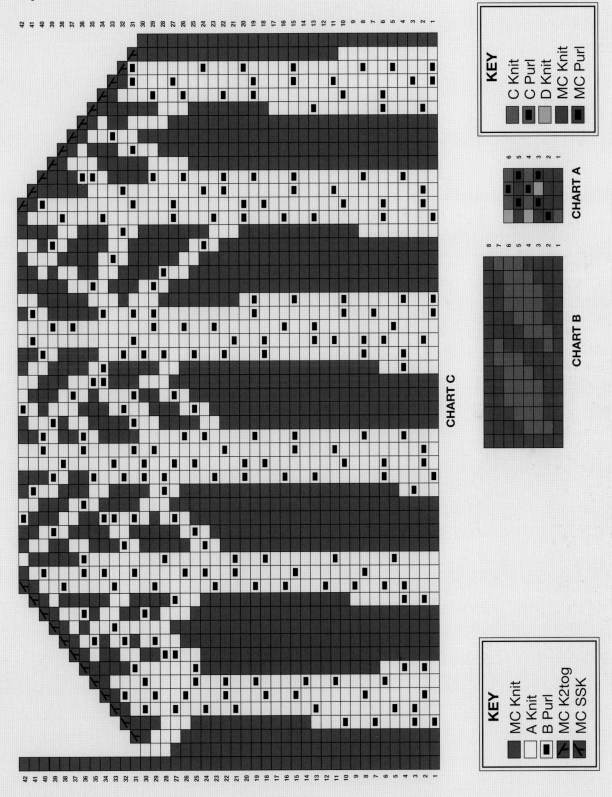

CHART C

CHART A

CHART B

KEY
- C Knit
- C Purl
- D Knit
- MC Knit
- MC Purl

KEY
- MC Knit
- A Knit
- B Purl
- MC K2tog
- MC SSK

CHAPTER 5

Swedish Celebrations

Two little girls in costume at Laknäs, Dalarne, Sweden, August 1, 1914.
AMERICAN SWEDISH INSTITUTE COLLECTION

In Sweden, knitted items go hand in hand with celebrations, and the patterns in this chapter honor that tradition. The Lucia Pillows commemorate Santa Lucia Day on December 13. Children throughout Sweden look forward to this date, which kicks off the holiday season with song and sweet treats. Our Dala Horse Garland honor the ever-popular carved red horse, a symbol of Sweden and a favorite decoration during Christmas time. But it is the All Things Swedish Shawl that is the quintessential knitter's project, celebrating the many traditions of Sweden in knitted stitches. Our favorite: the pattern that represents Swedish meatballs, the quintessential Swedish food.

Lucia Pillows

As adults, we are very lucky to have the opportunity to return to our youth through memory. Designing these pillows carried us back to our childhood memories of the first time each of us helped put up the traditional family Christmas tree. We can both remember placing our first ornament, ever so gently, in just the right place on the tree. And we remember holiday baking with our mothers and grandmothers. All of our Christmas memories are like the motifs on these pillows, a collection of the things we never want to forget.

The Lucia Pillows include the following motifs: crowns, which represent the love of the King and Queen of Sweden; Santa Lucia Girls and Star Boys, for the celebration of the traditional Santa Lucia Day on December 13; hearts, which feature prominently in Swedish folk art, symbolize love of country; the flowers, commonly used in Swedish embroidery, represent the beauty of the Swedish countryside; the Dala horse, which originated in the 1700s, is a traditional toy carved for children at holiday times; and Santa Lucia buns, which have two raisins in each one and are traditionally served on Santa Lucia Day.

We hope that while knitting the motifs on these pillows, you will dig out those old memories and share them with the children in your lives.

Finished Measurements
14"/35.5cm by 14"/35.5cm

Materials

- Blackberry Ridge Mermade Medium Weight 5-ply yarn, 100% machine washable wool, 114g/4oz, 215yds/197m:
- *Girl*: Old Rose (MC) or *Boy*: Cobalt Blue (MC), 1 skein each
- Lemon (A), Red (B), Nectarine (C), Cream (D), 1 skein each
- Cascade 220, 100% wool, 100g/3.5oz, 220yds/201m:
- Peach #9492 (E) and Lime #8910 (F), 1 skein each
- Size 7 (4.5mm), 16"/40.5cm long circular needle or size to obtain gauge
- Waste yarn
- Tapestry needle
- Stitch marker
- Pillow form, 14"/35.5cm by 14"/35.5cm (1 for each pillow)
- Small buttons for Santa Lucia Buns motif (5)
- Star button for Star Boy motif (5)

Gauge
17 sts and 22 rnds = 4"/10cm in St st.
Adjust needle as necessary to obtain correct gauge.

This iron candle holder, which we fondly nicknamed "Crowndalabra," fueled the design for the Lucia Pillows. We were especially drawn to the crowns around the edge of the piece.
AMERICAN SWEDISH
INSTITUTE COLLECTION

The Lucia Pillow, boy (top) and girl (bottom) versions.

Special Techniques

Provisional Cast-On (see Special Techniques Used, page 140)
Kitchener Stitch (see Special Techniques Used, page 140)

Pattern Note

Both pillows are designed to be worked in the round. For each row of the chart, follow front chart, reading right to left across all 61 sts, p1, then work the back chart from right to left over 61 sts, before moving on to the next row.

Instructions

Using provisional cast-on and waste yarn, CO 120 sts. Change to MC for either boy or girl pillow. Pm at beg of rnd and join, being careful not to twist sts.
Foll chosen chart, working Rows 1–78 once.
Using Kitchener stitch, close top together. Block pillow.

EMBROIDERY AND EMBELLISHING

For Girl's Pillow: Using Lazy Daisy stitch, make flowers with D. Create center of flower by making French knots using Boy's MC.
With C, make Lazy Daisy flames for candles.
With A, cut two 8"/20.5cm pieces of yarn. Using picture as a guide, thread these two pieces through 1 st. Braid 1–1.5"/2.5–4cm long, tie off, and cut off extra yarn. (**Note:** We made a regular three-strand braid and held together two strands as one for one of the three strands.) Rep for all Santa Lucia motifs.
Remove provisional cast-on, stuff, and Kitchener stitch closed.
Weave in all ends.

Cord

With B, make a twisted cord approximately 64"/162.5cm long (use Twisted Cord Directions sidebar from page 136 of *Norwegian Handknits* with this pattern). Using seams and side edges as guides, sew twisted cord to pillow. You will want to leave a 9"/23cm or longer tail both before you start and when you end to use for tying bow.

For Boy's Pillow: Sew small buttons in place for Santa Lucia Buns. Using picture as guide, sew star buttons to Star Boy's chest.
With B, cut two 8"/20.5cm pieces of yarn. Using picture as a guide, thread these two pieces through 1 st. Braid 1–1.5"/2.5–4cm long, tie off, and cut off extra yarn. **Note:** We made a regular three-strand braid and held together two strands as one for one of the three strands. Rep for tails on all Dala horse motifs.
Remove provisional cast-on, stuff, and Kitchener stitch closed.
Weave in all ends.

Cord

With B, make four twisted cord lengths with each finished measurement of approximately 20"/51cm long. Using seams and side edges as guides, sew one to each side, leaving extra length at each end to use to tie knots as decoration. Trim cord as desired.

Lucia Pillows Charts

LUCIA PILLOWS BOY FRONT CHART

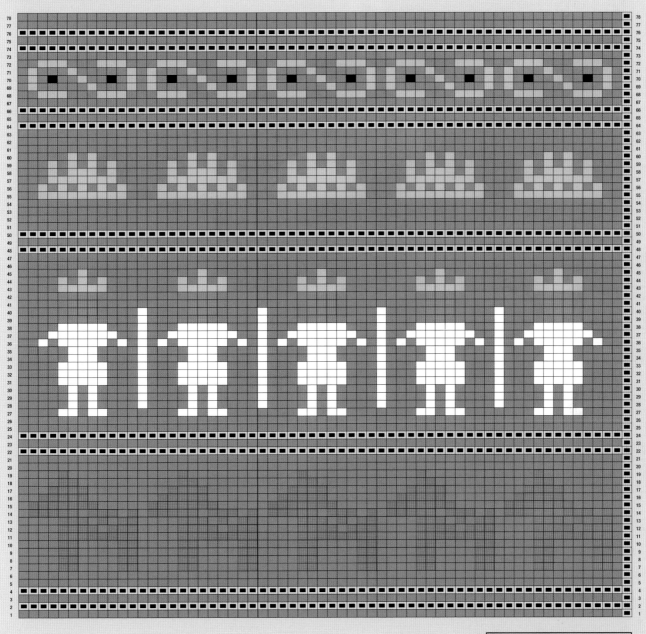

KEY	
	Cobalt Blue (MC)
	Red
	Cream
	Nectarine (C)
	Peach 9492
▪	Cream Purl
■	Button

LUCIA PILLOWS BOY BACK CHART

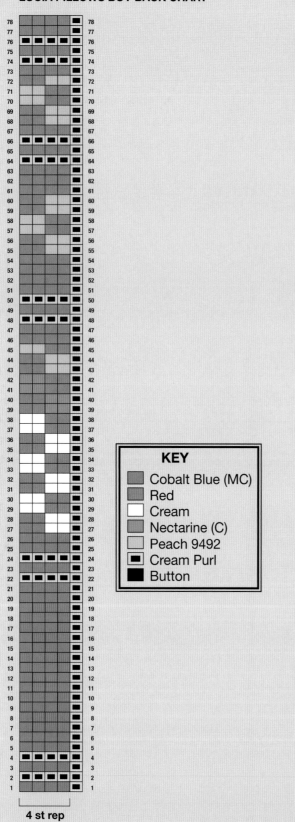

4 st rep

KEY
- Cobalt Blue (MC)
- Red
- Cream
- Nectarine (C)
- Peach 9492
- ■ Cream Purl
- ■ Button

LUCIA PILLOWS GIRL BACK CHART

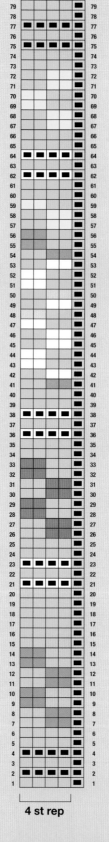

4 st rep

KEY
- Old Rose (MC)
- Lime 8910 (F)
- Red (B)
- Peach 9492 (E)
- Cream (D)
- Lemon (A)
- ■ Cream Purl
- ■ Button

LUCIA PILLOWS GIRL FRONT CHART

KEY	
☐	Old Rose (MC)
☐	Lime 8910 (F)
☐	Red (B)
☐	Peach 9492 (E)
☐	Cream (D)
☐	Lemon (A)
▪	Cream Purl
■	Button

All Things Swedish Shawl

Finished Measurements

72"/183cm by 27"/69cm

Materials

- Karabella Lace Merino,
  100% Merino wool,
  50g/1.75oz, 255yds/229m:
- Color 642, 9 skeins
- Size 2 (2.75mm), 24"/61cm
  long circular needle or size
  needed to obtain gauge
- Size 1 (2.25mm), 24"/61cm
  long circular needle (or
  1 size smaller than size
  needed to obtain gauge)
- Size C-2 (2.75mm) crochet
  hook
- Scandinavian braid
  (9 yds/8m)
- Buttons (24)
- Cotton sewing thread for
  sewing buttons into place
- Tapestry needle
- Waste yarn

Gauge

26 sts and 24 rows = 4"/10cm
in St st.
Adjust needle size as necessary to obtain correct gauge.

We wanted to include in this collection a shawl, something that exemplifies all things Swedish, with unique motifs and a touch of whimsy. Twelve eyelet sections divide the shawl into "stories" of pattern. When the shawl is completed, a Scandinavian braid is woven through the eyelets and held in place with a button on each end.

Special Techniques

Provisional Cast-On (see Special Techniques Used, page 00)

Instructions

**Using waste yarn and provisional cast on, CO 137 sts.
Eyelet pat:
Rows 1–4: Knit.
Row 5 (RS): K2, *yo, k2tog; rep from * to last st, sl 1 wyif.
Note: If you are including the Scandinavian braid in your shawl, then the eyelet number *must* be an odd number.
Rows 6–7: K.
Row 8: K, *increasing or decreasing* as next pat indicates for next section.
Note: After all eyelet sections are complete you should be ready to work a RS row.

Traditions in the Shawl

The first story told in the stitches of the All Things Swedish Shawl is of Santa Lucia Day, December 13. Traditionally, this day begins at dawn with a celebration of song that both warms and prepares the heart for the coming holidays. The candle flame motif represents the flames on the candles in the crown worn by the designated Santa Lucia. On each side of the candle flame motif are three Santa Lucia buns, the traditional treat eaten on this magical day.

The next story in the shawl represents weaving and the Swedish people's affinity for textile art. Any story collection would be incomplete without a crown motif. The Swedes have a great love for their King, Queen, and royal family, and this motif represents that sentiment. The row of hearts, a motif often found in Swedish embroidery and folk art, represents love of country and tradition. We designed the Swedish flag motif to show off the national pride of the Swedish people.

The middle section of the shawl is called "sunspots," representing midsummer in Sweden, when the sun doesn't set. This is also the section we fondly nicknamed the Swedish Meatball motif. For those of us unlucky ones who were not born Swedish, we get our first "taste" of Sweden through the gastronomic delight of this little morsel on a toothpick!

SANTA LUCIA CANDLES AND BUNS

To beg this section, you need 135 sts.

K4, work 9 sts of right-leaning Santa Lucia Bun motif, k4, work 5 reps of Candle Flame motif to equal 101 sts, k4, work 9 sts of left-leaning Santa Lucia Bun motif, k4.

Cont working charts as est, ending with a total of three Santa Lucia Buns on each side of 2 reps of Candle Flames.

Work 1 rep of Eyelet pat.

WOVEN MOTIF

On last row of Eyelet motif, dec 1 st across row—134 sts.

K 3 sts, work 8 reps of woven motif, k2, sl 1wyif.

Cont to foll chart for a total of 40 rows, ending with Row 8.

Work 1 rep of Eyelet pat.

CROWNS

On last row of Eyelet motif, inc 1 st across row—135 sts.

Set-up Row 1 (RS): K3, MC2, k2, work crown motif over 121 sts (6 reps plus 1), k2, MC2, k2, sl 1wyif.

Set-up Row 2 (WS): K1, p2, MC2, p2, work crown motif over 121 sts (6 reps plus 1), p2, MC2, p2, sl 1wyif.

Work as est over 24-row rep twice and Rows 1–12 once.

Work 1 rep of Eyelet pat.

HEARTS

To beg this section, you need 135 sts when starting Heart motif.

Set-up Row 1: K to last st, sl 1wyif.

Set-up Row 2: k1, p to last st, sl 1wyif.

Set-up Row 3: K3, *work Row 1 of Heart motif, k1; rep * across 5 motifs, k1, sl 1wyif.

Work Rows 1–17 of Heart motif once.

Ending Row: K1, p to last st, sl 1wyif.

Work 1 rep of Eyelet pat and on last row, inc 3 sts evenly across—138 sts.

SWEDISH FLAGS

To beg this section, you need 138 sts.

Set-up Row 1: K to Last st, sl 1wyif.

Set-up Row 2: K1, p to last st, sl 1wyif.

Set-up Rows 3 and 4: Rep set-up Rows 1 and 2.

Work Rows 1–12 of Flag motif fifteen times.**

Work 1 rep of Eyelet pat and on last row, dec 1 st—137 sts.

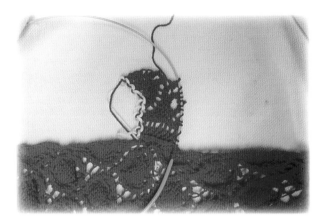

SUNSPOTS, A.K.A. MEATBALLS

To beg this section, you need 137 sts.

Work Sunspots Chart four and a half times (Rows 1–24 four times and Rows 1–10 once).

Work 1 rep of eyelet pat and on last row of inc 1 st—138 sts.

P 1 row.

Place sts on a holder.

Return to beg of instructions and rep from ** to **.

K 1 row.

P 1 row.

Place other half of shawl on smaller needle. Holding needles with WS's tog, use Kitchener st to join the two halves tog.

EDGING

Row 1: Sl 1, k1, (yo, k2tog) 2 times, (yo)3 times, k2tog, yo, p2tog.

Row 2: Yo, p2tog, k1, Sl first st to right needle dropping the other two wraps, place back on left needle, (k1, p1) two times all in large loop, (k1, p1) two times, k1, p2tog.

Row 3: Sl 1, (k1, yo, k2tog) two times, k4, yo, p2tog.

Row 4: Yo, p2tog, k5, p1, k2, p1, k1, p2tog.

Row 5: Sl 1, k1, yo, k2tog, k2, yo, k2tog, k3, yo, p2tog.

Row 6: Yo, p2tog, k4, p1, k3, p1, k1, p2tog.

Row 7: Sl 1, k1, yo, k2tog, k3, yo, k2tog, k2, yo, p2tog.

Row 8: Yo, p2tog, k3, p1, k4, p1, k1, p2tog.

Row 9: Sl 1, k1, yo, k2tog, k4, yo, k2tog, k1, yo, p2tog.

Row 10: Yo, p2tog, k2, p1, k5, p1, k1, p2tog.

Row 11: Sl 1, k1, yo, k2tog, k5, yo, k2tog, yo, p2tog.

Row 12: BO 3 sts, sl the st from right needle back to left needle, yo, p2tog, k5, p1, k1, p2tog.

CORNER OF EDGING

Place st marker 3 sts in from the corner of your picked-up edging sts and place marker 3 sts after the corner of your picked-up edging sts.

Work in edging pat to first marker.

*Work an even row as usual, except do not end with p2tog; instead, end with p1.

Work next odd row as usual.

Work next even row as usual.

Work next odd row as usual.*

Work from * to *, removing markers as you get to them.

Cont edging pat to 3 sts before next corner, repeating directions for placing markers and turning corners a total of four times around shawl.

FINISHING

Weave in all ends. Block.

Weave Scandinavian braid through eyelet pat, being careful not to pull braid too tightly. Use a button to hold braid down.

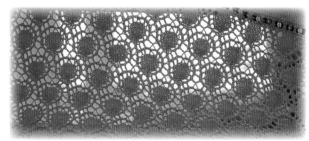

A Little Piece of Scandinavia, Right in the Twin Cities

Ingebretsen's, the ninety-year-old Scandinavian gift shop and meat market on East Lake Street in Minneapolis, Minnesota, is nothing short of tradition personified.

Charles Ingebretsen Sr. opened this iconic business in 1921, calling it Model Meat Market. The Lake Street store was actually Ingebretsen's second location, but its proximity to the trolley car line made it more popular than the original Riverside Avenue shop. After World War II, Ingebretsen's son, Charles Jr., known as "Bud," began to manage the store. Bud soon found a partner, Warren Dahl, who brought with him the recipe for Swedish meatball mix that has since become legendary.

Ingebretsen's, which now includes a gift shop and needlework store, remains in the family. Bud's daughter, Julie Ingebretsen, has been with the store since 1974, when she agreed to manage the then-new gift shop. Turns out, she thought she might stay awhile. Over the years, Julie has transformed the gift shop from a mere place to linger while waiting for food orders to a popular shopping destination, offering a high-quality selection of Scandinavian books, culinary supplies, glass and dishware, jewelry, and surprises. The shop has become such a favorite stop during the holiday season that it's not uncommon to see a line out the door.

As enticing as the gifts may be, if you can make your way through the gift shop to the meat department you will be rewarded in the end. Ahhh, the meat department.

The lefse, lutefisk, lingonberry jam, potato sausage, and the much-loved, much-sought-after Swedish meatball mix all await as you step into the meat department and, ultimately, back in time. The meat department, managed by Warren Dahl's son, Steve, still uses old meat counter cases that harken back to a time when it was commonplace to stop at the bakery for a loaf of bread, have milk and dairy delivered to the door by a man in a white uniform, and, of course, purchase meat at the local, trusted butcher shop.

Buy all the sausage, lefse, and jam you want; just don't bother asking for the recipe for those famous Swedish meatballs. We've often heard customers ask for it, only to hear the friendly reply: "How much can I get for you today?" Nevermind. Just pick up a batch of the mix and move on.

Before you leave, be sure to stop by the wonderful needlework shop, located in the adjacent storefront. This is the place to find the best Scandinavian yarns, knitting patterns, cross-stitch kits, tatting supplies, and ready-to-wear Scandinavian clothing. Ingebretsen's needlework department also has a classroom, a children's section, and an encouraging, fun, and friendly staff who are happy to answer your needlework questions.

We encourage any and all to stop at Ingebretsen's, buy a piece of glassware, a kit from the needlework department, and some Swedish meatball mix. Out-of-towners can shop via their website, www.ingebretsens.com. You won't be disappointed!

SWEDISH SHAWL CANDLES CHART

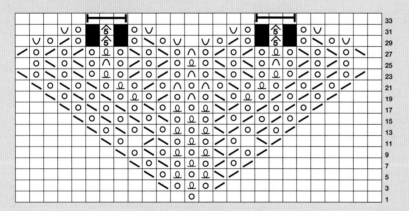

SWEDISH LACE HEART CHART

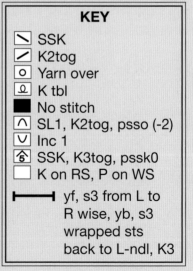

KEY

◢	SSK
◥	K2tog
o	Yarn over
⋀	SL1, K2tog, psso (-2)
□	K on RS, P on WS

even rows 2-36: K1, P
across to last st, SL1wyif

KEY

◢	SSK
◥	K2tog
o	Yarn over
Ω	K tbl
■	No stitch
⋀	SL1, K2tog, psso (-2)
∨	Inc 1
Ⓢ	SSK, K3tog, pssk0
□	K on RS, P on WS
⊢——⊣	yf, s3 from L to R wise, yb, s3 wrapped sts back to L-ndl, K3

SWEDISH CROWNS CHART

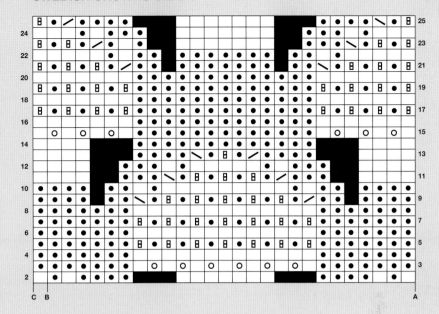

KEY
- ⟍ SSK
- ⟋ K2tog
- ○ Yarn over
- • P on RS, K on WS
- ■ No stitch
- ☐ K on RS, P on WS
- 𐅂 K1tbl (K1 through back loop)
- ⌒ SL1, y0, K1, PSLS0

⌒³ Mock Cable (MC2) over 2 sts
₂

20 + 1

SWEDISH FLAG CHART

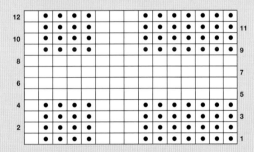

KEY
- • P on RS, K on WS
- ☐ K on RS, P on WS

Multiple 15

SWEDISH SUNSPOTS CHART

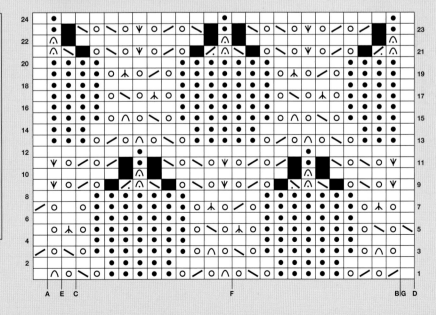

KEY
- ⟍ SSK
- ⟋ K2tog
- ○ Yarn over
- • P on RS, K on WS
- ■ No stitch
- ⋀ SL1, K2tog, psso (-2)
- ⌃ P3tog
- Ψ KPK tbl (+2)
- ⟋ P2tog
- ⊼ S2KP2
- ☐ K on RS, P on WS

OLD SWEDISH RECIPE

SWEDISH MEATBALLS

No, this isn't the recipe for Ingebretsen's famous Swedish Meatballs, but it's pretty good nonetheless. The meatballs can be made ahead of time, refrigerated, and then reheated before serving.

1 c. minced onion

4 tbsp. butter

2 ½ lbs. meat loaf mixture (ground beef, pork and veal)

1 c. fresh bread crumbs

3 eggs, slightly beaten

1 ½ c. half and half

2 tsp. salt

¼ tsp. pepper

¼ tsp. ground nutmeg

¼ tsp. ground allspice

¼ tsp. ground cardamom

½ tsp. dried dill weed

vegetable oil cooking spray

⅓ c. flour

2 (10 ½ oz.) cans beef broth

1 c. whipping cream

½ tsp. dried dill weed

Preheat the oven to 400°F. In a small skillet, cook onion in 1 tablespoon of butter until soft. In large bowl, combine onion with next ten ingredients (mixture will be very soft). Shape into 1 ½-inch balls, arrange on jellyroll pan lightly sprayed with vegetable oil cooking spray. Bake for 14–16 minutes, or until cooked through and lightly browned. Meanwhile, melt 3 tablespoons of butter in a large skillet; stir in flour. Gradually whisk in beef broth. Cook over medium heat, stirring constantly, until mixture thickens. Stir in whipping cream and ½ teaspoon of dill weed; simmer 5 minutes. (Have gravy finished when meatballs come out of the oven.) Scrape meatballs and browned bits into gravy, stirring to combine. These can be refrigerated and reheated at 325°F for 40–50 minutes.

SHAWL WEAVE PATTERN CHART

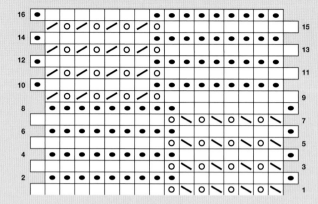

KEY

◣ SSK	● P on RS, K on WS
◢ K2tog	☐ K on RS, P on WS
○ Yarn over	

SANTA LUCIA BUNS CHART

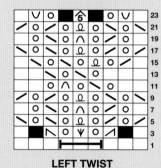

LEFT TWIST

RIGHT TWIST

KEY

◣ SSK	ⱽ KPK tbl +2
◢ K2tog	⋀ SL1, K2tog, psso (-2)
○ Yarn over	⋁ Inc 1
℧ K tbl	⑤ SSK, K3tog, pssko (-4)
◿ K3tog	◺ K3tog tbl
◼ No stitch	☐ K on RS, P on WS

⊢━━┤ yf, sl 3 sts from L to R need 6 p-wise, yb, sl 3 wrapped sts back to L needle, k3

even rows 2-24: K1, P across to last st, SL1wyif

ala Horse Garland

Finished Measurements
Horse Width: 2"/5cm
Horse Height: 3"/7.5cm

Materials

2 FINE

- Cascade 220 Superwash Sport,100% superwash Merino wool, 50g/1.75oz, 136yds/124m:
- Red #809 (MC), 1 skein
- Small amounts of Yellow #820 (A), Mint #1942 (B), Teal #845 (C), #803 Navy (D)
- Size 2 (2.75mm) double-pointed needles or size needed to obtain gauge
- Small size crochet hook
- Tapestry needle

Gauge
24 sts and 32 rows = 4"/10cm in St st.
Adjust needle size as necessary to obtain correct gauge.

The distinctive style of folk painting called *Dalmälning* originated in the province of Dalarna, Sweden. The Dalarna folk painting was first practiced in churches as a form of decorative storytelling. The painting style, which was originally used to teach Bible stories to parishioners, evolved into a means of commemorating important events like weddings.

The migration of the painting style to the carved horse is said to have started when a Dala painter, Stlkä Eric Hansson, was disabled. Since he was no longer able to paint walls, he sold the painted horses to help support his family. The carved horse with the "fancy flower painting" has been adopted as a symbol of Sweden.

Special Techniques
Kitchener Stitch (see Special Techniques Used, page 140)

Instructions

First Leg
With MC, CO 12 sts. Pm at beg of rnd and join, taking care not to twist sts.

Lazy Daisy, step 1.

Lazy Daisy, step 2.

French knot.

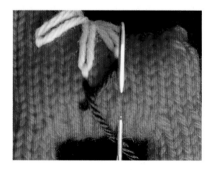

Zigzag stitch.

Rnds 1–12: Knit.
Rnd 13: BO 2 sts, k to end.
Place rem 10 sts on holder.

Second Leg

Work same as first leg, leaving sts on needles.

Belly

With MC, CO 7 sts for belly at end of last needle, place sts from first leg onto needles and knit them, CO 7 more sts for belly, and cont to k5 sts from second leg, joining to form a circle—34 sts. Pm here for center back and beg of rnd.

Note: The opening that was created by the CO sts and the leg BO is for stuffing the horse.

Body

Rnds 1–9: Knit.
Rnd 10: K1, ssk, k to within 3 sts from end, k2tog, k—32 sts.
Rnd 11: Knit. Fold in half at center back marker and, using Kitchener stitch, weave 14 sts tog (7 sts from each side) to form back of horse. Keep marker at center back.
Rnd 12: K9, at center front CO 10 sts, k to end—28 sts. **Note**: The hole that forms on the center back will be covered up with an embroidered flower later.
Rnd 13: Knit.
Rnd 14: K1, ssk, k10, k1f&b of next 2 sts, k10 , k2tog, k1—28 sts.
Rnd 15: K13, k1f&b of next 2 sts, k13—30 sts.
Rnd 16: K1, ssk, k24 , k2tog, k1—28 sts.
Rnd 17: Knit.
Rnd 18: K1, ssk, k9, k2tog, ssk, k9, k2tog, k1—24 sts.
Rnd 19: K10, k2tog, ssk, k10—22 sts.
Rnd 20: K1, ssk, k6, k2tog, ssk, k6, k2tog, k1—18 sts.
Rnd 21: K7, k2tog, ssk, k7—16 sts.
Rnd 22: K1, ssk, k3, k2tog, ssk, k3, k2tog, k1—12 sts.
Rnd 23: K4, k2tog, ssk, k4—10 sts.
Rnd 24: K1, ssk, k2tog, ssk, k2tog, k1—6 sts.
Rnds 25–26: Knit, thread rem sts onto yarn, and pull tight for ear. Sew chin and leg openings closed, stuff with fiberfill, and sew belly. Weave in all ends.

GARLAND CORD

With double strand of D and dpns, CO 4 sts, knit, *without turning work, slide sts to other end of needle, knit, rep from * for approximately 64"/162.5cm.

FINISHING

With A, B, or C, work one Lazy Daisy stitch on the back of the horse. With an alternating color, make three or four French knots in the center of flower. With C or D, work zigzag stitch around horse for harness. Cut 12"/30.5cm strands of A and D. Thread one strand of A and D through center neck, braid, and use ends to attach horse to Garland Cord.

The Famous Dala Horse

By Harley Refsal

Harley Refsal, a second-generation Norwegian American, is an acclaimed woodcarver who teaches carving at Luther College in Decorah, Iowa, and around the world. Refsal is credited with reviving the almost lost tradition of Scandinavian wood carving and has written many books on the subject, including Art & Technique of Scandinavian-style Woodcarving *(2004) and* Whittling Little Folk: 20 Delightful Characters to Carve and Paint *(2011), both published by Fox Chapel Publishing.*

Anyone who has ever visited Sweden or the Swedish-settled communities in North America recognizes that the Dala horse is the unofficial, but widely popular symbol of Sweden. The dear old horses have been carved as toys and gifts for children and grandchildren for centuries throughout Scandinavia and in other parts of the world. In the preindustrial era, when a large percentage of the Swedish population lived on farms, the family horses were some of the most essential animals on the farm.

In about 1840, when commercial logging operations got going in heavily wooded central Sweden, large numbers of men headed off into the woods after Christmas each year to cut trees for the recently established sawmills, which were busy producing lumber for a rapidly industrializing European continent. And what did many of those men do during their long, dark winter evenings, while packed into their cramped bunkhouses?

They carved Dala horses. When the men returned home in the spring, they gave the Dala horses to the kids as gifts. The carved horses grew in popularity, and became even more popular when artists began to decorate the horses with paint, often drawing their design inspiration from painted wall murals in churches or public buildings.

Within a century after loggers began to carve Dala horses, the now much-loved horses were known throughout the country. In 1939, the little painted horse from Dalarna galloped onto the world stage as well, appearing in the gift shop of the Swedish Pavilion at the World's Fair in New York City. The Dala horse was an immediate hit, and its fame spread far and wide.

And what staying power! Today the Dala horse is not just a child's toy or a symbol of Sweden and Swedish handwork. It's also become a palette, a canvas on which to celebrate themes of all kinds. Take for instance *Dalapalooza*, a project in which woodcarver Harley Refsal carved a couple hundred horses and gave a matched pair to artists and friends from around the country and abroad to decorate in whatever way they chose. Upon completion, Refsal gets one of the horses returned to him to add to his ever-increasing herd, which now numbers nearly one hundred. The American Swedish Institute in Minneapolis has undertaken a similar project, *Dalahorse Dialogue*, which will feature Refsal-carved horses decorated by a wide variety of artists from around the country and around the corner.

If only those 1840s farmer/loggers from Dalarna could see just how famous their little wooden horses have become!

Size
Adult's Average

Finished Measurements
Circumference: 7 ½"/19cm
Height: 5 ½"/14cm

Materials

- Cascade 220 Superwash Sport, 100% superwash Merino wool, 50g/1.75oz, 136yds/124m:
- Blue #813 (MC), Ginger #858 (A), Black #815 (B), Red #809 (C), Taupe #873 (D), Cream #817 (E), 1 skein each
- Sizes 3 (3.25mm) and 5 (3.75mm) double-pointed needles or size needed to obtain gauge
- Size F-5 (3.75mm) crochet hook
- Stitch marker

Gauge
28 sts and 32 rnds = 4"/10cm in St st on larger needles. *Adjust needles as necessary to obtain correct gauge.*

Tomten Wristers

These wristers celebrate the folklore of the Swedish Tomte, mythical little men who take care of the farmstead. The name *Tomte* means "homestead man." The little man is child-sized and usually wears old clothes and a bright red hat. The Tomte take credit for clean and orderly farmsteads, although they still will cause mischief if denied their due of Christmas porridge.

The design for the bearded man is from a weaving made by Maj-Britt Westerberg. Westerberg's weaving is a traditional pattern from the Swedish area of Jamtland that features two styles of figures: one is the bearded man, and the other is a woman. The woman figure could also be easily adapted for a second wrister, creating a his-and-her set of wristers.
AMERICAN SWEDISH INSTITUTE COLLECTION

Instructions

With smaller dpns and MC, CO 60 sts. Pm for beg of rnd and join, taking care not to twist sts.

Rnd 1: Purl.

Rnd 2: *In one st k 5 sts wrapping yarn twice around needle (k1, yo, k1, yo, k1, yo, k1, yo, k1); rep from * around.

Rnd 3: *Slip each of the 5 double-wrapped sts onto the right needle dropping second wrap as they are slipped; return 5 long sts to left needle and p all 5 sts tog, p9, rep from * around—60 sts.

Rnd 4: *K1, ssk, k5, k2tog; rep from* around—48 sts.

Rnd 5: Purl.

Break off MC. Change to larger dpns.

Rnds 6–36: Work Chart A in St st, changing colors as indicated.

Break off A, B, C, D, and E. Change to small dpns.

Rnds 37–41: Attach MC, work around in k1, p1 rib.

Work crochet picot BO as foll: with crochet hook in right hand and needle in left hand, *using crochet hook, BO 4 sts, chain 3; rep from * around.

Break yarn and secure ends.

FINISHING

Weave in all ends.

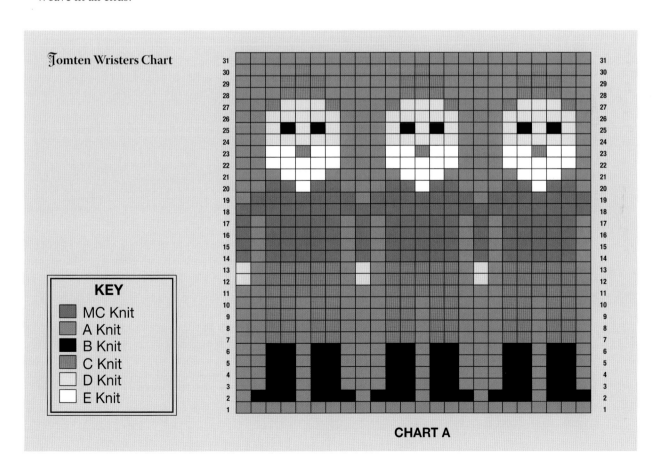

Jomten Wristers Chart

KEY

- MC Knit
- A Knit
- B Knit
- C Knit
- D Knit
- E Knit

CHART A

Daisy Top

The inspiration for this design comes from the bodice of the Swedish National Costume: a blue twill vest with metal eyelets for lacing the bodice, which was decorated with white daisies and green stems. The vest and bodice were worn over a plain white shirt and a colored skirt with a daisy border.

This top is modeled after the vest, but includes a row of daisies along the bottom as a reminder of the border on the skirt. It is knit in a beautiful linen-cotton blend that gives the piece an heirloom feel. The background stitch on the top is a modified linen stitch, which is reminiscent of hand-woven linen fabric.

Special Techniques

Kitchener Stitch (see Special Techniques Used, page 140)

Sweden's National Costume

Regional dress was common in the rural Swedish society, where a large percentage of the people earned their living from farming. Each area had a specific style, and the clothes they wore identified the people of each region. This regional identity was lost, to some extent, in the industrialization of Sweden. By the 1870s, folk costumes were disappearing.

Encouraged by a folk art revival movement, Märta Jörgensen designed the original Swedish national costume in 1903. The First World War, however, quickly subdued the movement. Märta was proud of her design and wore the costume at every special event until her death in 1967. It was not until June 6, 1983, when Queen Silvia wore the costume to Sweden's first National Day celebration, that Märta's costume was accepted as the official national costume.

Actress-singer Olga Lindgren Nilsen owned the costume that was on display at the ASI. She wore it throughout Swedish-America, whenever she performed song, dance, and folk comedy routines in the Swedish language.

Pattern Stitches

Linen Stitch (worked in-the-rnd):
Rnd 1: *K1, yf, sl 1, yb; rep from * around.
Rnd 2: Knit.
Rnd 3: *Yf, sl 1, yb, k1; rep from * around.
Rnd 4: Knit.
Rep Rnds 1–4 for Linen St (worked-in-rnd).

Linen Stitch (worked back and forth):
Row 1: *K1, yf, sl 1, yb; rep from * across.
Row 2: Purl.
Row 3: *Yf, sl 1, yb, k1; rep from * across.
Row 4: Purl.
Rep Rows 1–4 for Linen St (worked back and forth).

Instructions

With MC, CO 240 (270, 300, 330) sts. Pm and join, taking care not to twist sts.

BORDER
Work Chart A (lace pat) for 7 rnds.
Next Rnd: *K13, k2tog; rep from * around—224 (252, 280, 308) sts.
Attach A and work Chart B (border pat) for 6 rnds. Break off A.
Attach B and work Chart C (daisy pat) for 14 rnds. Break off B.
Attach A and work Chart B (border pat) for 6 rnds. Break off A.

BODY

Work Linen st in-the-rnd until piece measures 15 (16, 17, 18)"/38 (40.5, 43, 45.5)cm from CO edge, ending after an odd rnd.

DIVIDE FOR BODICE

Using waste yarn to hold sts (or stitch holders), divide work as folls: 6 (6, 9, 9) sts for armhole, 50 (57, 61, 68) sts for right front, 50 (57, 61, 68) sts for left front, 12 (12, 18, 18) sts for armhole, 100 (114, 122, 136) sts for back, 6 (6, 9, 9) sts for armhole—224 (252, 280, 308) sts.
Note: The remainder of the top will be worked back and forth (flat) in Linen st.

BACK ARMHOLE SHAPING

Turn work so that inside (WS) is facing and purl 100 (114, 122, 136) back sts.

Reestablish the Linen st pat working back and forth in rows; at the same time, work Dec Row every other row for 12 rows, then every 4th row for 24 rows as foll:
Dec Row (RS): K1, ssk, work Linen st as est until 3 sts from end, k2tog, k1. Cont on rem 76 (90, 98, 112) sts until 7 (7 ½, 7 ½, 8)"/18 (19, 19, 20.5)cm from beg of armhole, ending with a WS row.

BACK NECK SHAPING

With RS facing, leaving first 30 (35, 37, 42) sts on needle for right back, place next 16 (20, 24, 28) sts on a holder for center back neck, then place last 30 (35, 37, 42) sts on a holder for left back.

Right Back Neck Shaping

Row 1: Work Linen st to within 3 sts from end, k2tog, k1.
Row 2: P1, p2tog-tbl, work Linen st to end.
Rows 3–12: Rep Rows 1 and 2, five more times—18 (23, 25, 30) sts.
Rows 13–14: Cont even in Linen st for 2 rows.
Row 15: Work Linen st to within 2 sts from end, k2tog, k1.
Row 16: Cont even in Linen st.
Rows 17–26: Rep Rows 13–16 five more times—12 (17, 19, 24) sts.

Right Shoulder Short Rows

Row 1 (RS): Cont in Linen st.
Row 2: Work 8 (12, 12, 16) sts, sl 1, yf, sl st back, turn and work back.
Row 3: Work 4 (6, 6, 8) sts, sl 1, yf, sl st back, turn and work back.
Place sts on holder.

Left Back Neck Shaping

Place 30 (35, 37, 42) left back sts from holder onto needle.
Row 1 (RS): K1, k2tog-tbl, cont Linen st to end.
Row 2: Work Linen st to within 3 sts from end, p2tog, k1.
Rows 3–12: Rep Rows 1 and 2 five more times—18 (23, 25, 30) sts
Rows 13–14: Cont in Linen st.
Row 15: K1, k2tog-tbl, cont Linen st to end.

Row 16: Cont in Linen st.

Rows 17–16: Rep Rows 13–16 five more times—12 (17, 19, 24) sts.

Left Shoulder Short Rows

Row 1 (RS): Work 8 (12, 12, 16) sts, sl 1, yf, sl st back, turn and work back.

Row 2: Work 4 (6, 6, 8) sts, sl 1, yf, sl st back, turn and work back. Place sts on holder.

RIGHT FRONT ARMHOLE SHAPING

Place 50 (57, 61, 68) right front sts from holder onto needle, attach yarn at center front, and purl row on WS.

Dec Row: K1, k2tog-tbl, cont Linen st to end.

Next Row: Cont in Linen st.

Rep Dec Row every other row for ten more rows, then every fourth row for 24 rows—38 (45, 49, 56) sts.

RIGHT FRONT NECK SHAPING

Work Linen st over the next 30 (35, 37, 42) sts; place rem 8 (10, 12, 14 sts) on holder for neckline.

Row 1: P1, p2tog-tbl, cont Linen st to end.

Row 2: Work Linen st to within 3 sts from end, k2tog, k1.

Rows 3–12: Rep Rows 1 and 2 five more times—18 (23, 25, 30) sts.

Rows 13–14: Cont in Linen st.

Row 15: Work to within 3 sts from end, k2tog, k1.

Row 16: Cont in Linen st.

Rows 17–26: Rep Rows 13–16 five more times.

Cont on rem 12 (17, 19, 24) sts until armhole is same length as outside edge of back armhole opening.

RIGHT SHOULDER SHORT ROWS

Row 1: Cont in Linen st.

Row 2: Work 8 (12, 12, 16) sts, sl 1, yf, sl st back, turn and work back.

Row 3: Work 4 (6, 6, 8) sts, sl 1, yf, sl st back, turn and work back. Place sts on holder.

Using Kitchener stitch, join right front and right back shoulders.

LEFT FRONT ARMHOLE SHAPING

Work same as Right Front Armhole Shaping to neck shaping, rev shaping.

LEFT FRONT NECK SHAPING

Work same as Right Front Neck, rev shaping.

LEFT SHOULDER SHORT ROWS

Row 1: Work 8 (12, 12, 16) sts, sl 1, yf, sl st back, turn and work back.

Row 2: Work 4 (6, 6, 8) sts, sl 1, yf, sl st back, turn and work back. Place sts on holder.

Using Kitchener stitch, join left front and left back shoulders.

OLD SWEDISH RECIPE

SWEDISH HARDTACK

Swedish hardtack, or *knäckebröd* in Swedish, is a biscuit-like cracker that is relatively easy to make. Try it with cheese, butter, or lingonberry jam.

1 c. + 1 tbsp. flour

¼ tsp. baking soda

¼ tsp. salt

2 tbsp. sugar

½ c. buttermilk

2 tbsp. unsalted butter (1/4 stick), melted

Sesame seeds

In a medium bowl, combine dry ingredients. Add buttermilk and melted butter and stir until smooth. Refrigerate mixture for 1–2 hours. Meanwhile, preheat oven to 350°F. Using 1 tablespoon of dough, roll out thin on floured board. Sprinkle liberally with sesame seeds. Use a pizza cutter to cut into triangles. Bake on an ungreased cookie sheet for 10–25 minutes, or until lightly brown. Do not underbake. Store in an airtight container.

ARMHOLE EDGING

Place 6 (6, 9, 9) underarm sts from holder onto shorter circular needle, then with MC pick up and k90 (90, 91, 91) sts around armhole—96 (96, 100, 100) sts. Pm and join.

Rnd 1: Purl.

Rnds 2–3: *K2 with MC, k2 with A; rep from * around.

Rnd 4: Purl.

Rnds 5–7: Knit.

BO. Fold facing over along Rnd 4 purl ridge and sew to inside edge.

NECK FACING

Place 8 (10, 12, 14) neck sts from holder onto shorter circular needle, then with MC pick up and k37 sts around neck to back; work 16 (20, 24, 28) sts from holder for center back, cont to pick up and k37 sts around neckline, work front 8 (10, 12, 14) sts from other side of neck—106 (114, 122, 130) sts.

Rnd 1: Knit.

Rnd 2: *K2 with MC, k2 with A; rep from *, end k2 MC.

Rnd 3: *P2 with MC, p2 with A; rep from *, end p2 MC.

Rnds 4–5: Purl.

Rnd 6: Knit.

Rnd 7: Purl.

BO. Fold facing over along Rnd 4 purl ridge and sew to inside edge.

NECKLINE

With A, knit applied I-cord around the neck slit. For eyelet holes, work 3 rnds of unattached I-cord, skip 3 rnds, then work 3 rnds of attached I-cord and so on, evenly spacing the eyelet holes along the slit.

EMBROIDERY

With C, make a cluster of French knots inside each daisy around bottom of top.

With B, use the Lazy Daisy stitch to make three daisies on each side of front. Use the close-up photo as a guide for the placement of the flowers. For each leaf of flower make one large petal (Lazy Daisy) and one smaller petal inside the larger one. With C, make a cluster of French knots inside each flower. With A, use satin stitch to make two or three leaves around each daisy, making the edge of the leaf jagged by using long and short stitches.

LACE

With C, make an I-cord approx 36"/91.5 in length and lace through eyelets on neck slit.

FINISHING

Weave in all ends. Block.

𝔇aisy Top Chart

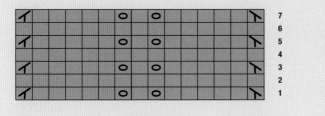

CHART A

CHART B

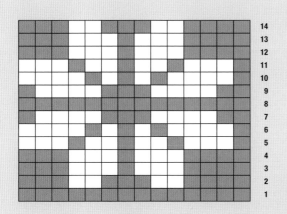

CHART C

KEY

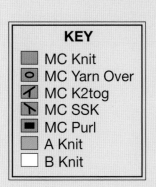

- MC Knit
- MC Yarn Over
- MC K2tog
- MC SSK
- MC Purl
- A Knit
- B Knit

SWEDISH DAISY TOP DIAGRAM

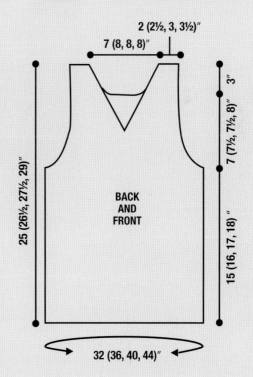

2 (2½, 3, 3½)″

7 (8, 8, 8)″

3″

7 (7½, 7½, 8)″

15 (16, 17, 18)″

25 (26½, 27½, 29)″

BACK
AND
FRONT

32 (36, 40, 44)″

Daisy Chain

Finished Measurements
Daisy circumference:
2 ½"/6.5cm
Length: 12"/30.5cm

Materials

- Louet MerLin, 60%
  linen/40% cotton in Fine/
  Sport Weight, 100g/3.5oz,
  250yds/228m:
- Willow #55 (A), Cream #30
  (B), Goldilocks #05 (C), 1
  skein each
- Size 2 (2.75mm) double-
  pointed needles
- Buttons (¼"/6mm) for
  flower centers (8)
- Tapestry needle

As a child, making daisy chains was a summer tradition. Picking the daisies, splitting the stems, and inserting the second flower through the previous stem made a wonderful chain. The chain could then be used as a crown or necklace, but its beauty was fleeting. Within a short time, the flowers wilted and the crown was tossed away. With this pattern, you can knit a long-lasting chain of daisies. Make as many daisy segments as you wish, and use the chain to dress up your favorite straw hat or as a long garland to decorate the house for Midsummer's Eve.

Pattern Notes
Gauge is not essential.
To knit the chain shown here, make eight flowers.

Knitted On Cast-On Step-by-Step

STEP 1: Insert needle into front of rem st.

STEP 2: Knit stitch and pull new loop though first st.

STEP 3: Place this newly form st onto left needle. Repeat steps 1–3 in the new st.

Instructions

FLOWER CENTER

With C, CO 6 sts. Knit seven rows. BO, leaving a 6"/15cm tail.
Using a sharp tapestry needle, run tail through all four edges and pull tight over a button; secure ends.

FLOWER PETALS

With A, CO 8 sts.
Row 1: Knit.
Row 2: BO all but one st. Use Knitted On CO to add 7 sts (8 sts total).
Row 3: Knit and BO all but one st.
Rep Rows 2 and 3 until there are twelve petals; BO on last petal, leaving 6"/15cm tail.
Using tapestry needle, run tail through the inner edge of petals and pull snug to make a ring. Sew petal ring to bottom of flower center; secure ends.

STEM AND LEAVES

With A, CO 4 sts; work I-cord for 6 rnds.
Knitted On CO 8 sts and knit back toward stem, k8, turn work, k8, turn work, BO 8 sts of leaf, resume I-cord for another 6 rnds. Rep from * to * for second leaf. Work additional 16 rnds of I-cord; break off, leaving a 6"/15cm tail. Gather remaining sts together and secure to stem by folding into loop and sewing end to stem. Sew CO end of stem to the underside of the flower.

Make eight flowers. To Chain, loop flower head through stem of next flower, cont with desired number of daisies.

Crayfish Hot Pad

Finished Measurements
20"/51cm circumference by 12"/30.5cm height (from top to tip of earflap)

Materials

• Cascade 220, 100% wool, 100g/3.5oz, 220yds/201m: #7818 Royal Blue (MC), 1 skein Cascade 220 Paints, 100% wool, 100g/3.5oz, 220yds/201m: #9868 Flame (CC), 1 skein
• Size 7 (4.5mm) 16"/40.5cm long circular needle or size needed to obtain gauge
• Crochet hook size G-6 (4mm)
• Stitch markers (2)

Gauge
20 sts and 28 rnds = 4"/10cm in St st.
Adjust needle size as necessary to obtain correct gauge.

The end of summer in Sweden is marked with an outdoor party featuring crayfish. The tradition of the crayfish feast or crayfish supper, held in the month of August, started in the mid-nineteenth century. In contrast to a Louisiana "crawdad" boil, Swedish crayfish are boiled with a mild dill flavor instead of the hot and spicy Cajun seasoning. The crayfish are boiled in a large pot over an open fire. It is perfectly acceptable, and in fact easier, to eat crayfish with your fingers, breaking off the tails, peeling, and eating. The crayfish feast is often accompanied with bread, cheese, beer, and schnapps.

The outdoor country setting of the crayfishing activities is depicted in the Carl Larsson's painting of the same name. In *Crayfishing*, Carl's family is shown collecting crayfish with a net in one hand and bait suspended from a line in the other hand. The Larsson children appear to be doing all this while balancing on a small rock on the shoreline or while wading in the water.

Special Techniques
Continental Cast-On (see Special Techniques Used, page 140)
Kitchener Stitch (see Special Techniques Used, page 140)
Fulling (see Special Techniques Used, page 140)

Pattern Notes

This hot pad is knit in the round as a tube and closed off at each end.
It can also be knit in double knitting; the result will be a reversible
positive-negative pattern.

Instructions

With MC, using continental cast-on with waste yarn, CO 106 sts.
Pm at beg of rnd and after 53 sts, then join, taking care not to twist sts.
Knit 1 rnd.

EST CHART

Attach CC and work Chart Rnds 1–66 in St st.
Break off CC. With MC only, knit 1 rnd.

FINISHING

Remove waste yarn from CO edge and place sts on needle. Using
Kitchener stitch, close top of pot holder. Weave in all ends.

Full (felt) the piece by washing in warm water with mild soap, then
agitate until it begins to look fuzzy. Dry flat.

Crayfish Hot Pad Chart

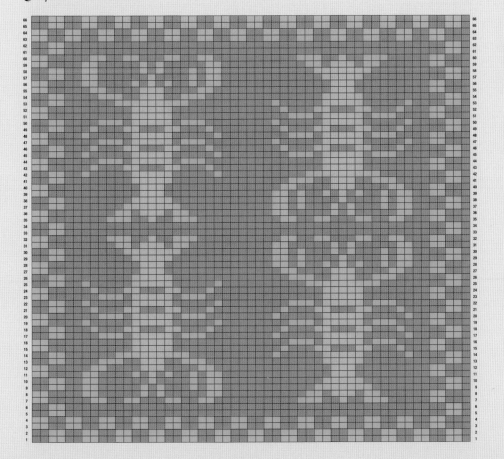

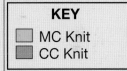

KEY

MC Knit
CC Knit

Abbreviations

beg . . . . begin, beginning, begins

BO . . . . bind off

CC . . . . contrast color

cm . . . . centimeter(s)

CO . . . . cast on

cont . . . . . . continue, continuing

dec(s) . . . . . decrease(s), decreasing

dpn . . . . double-pointed needle(s)

est . . . . establish, established

foll . . . . follow(s), following

inc(s) . . . . . increase(s), increasing

k . . . . knit

k1f&b . . . . . knit into front then back of same st (increase)

k1f,b,&f . . . knitting into front, back, then front again of same st (increase 2 sts)

k1-tbl . . . . . knit 1 st through back loop

k2tog . . . . . knit 2 sts together (decrease)

k2tog-tbl . . . knit 2 sts together through back loops

kwise . . . . . knitwise (as if to knit)

LH . . . . left-hand

m(s) . . . . . . marker(s)

MC . . . . main color

mm . . . . millimeter(s)

M1 . . . . make 1 (increase)

M1k . . . . . . make 1 knitwise

M1p . . . . . . make 1 purlwise

pat(s) . . . . . pattern(s)

p . . . . purl

p1f&b . . . . . purl into front then back of same st (increase)

p1-tbl . . . . . purl 1 st through back loop

p2tog . . . . . purl 2 sts together (decrease)

pm . . . . place marker

psso . . . . . . pass slip st(s) over

pwise . . . . . purlwise (as if to purl)

rem . . . . remain(s), remaining

rep(s) . . . . . repeat(s), repeated, repeating

rnd(s) . . . . . round(s)

RH . . . . right-hand

RS . . . . right side (of work)

revsc . . . . . . reverse single crochet (crab st)

sc . . . . single crochet

sl . . . . slip, slipped, slipping

ssk . . . . [slip 1 stknitwise] twice from left needle to right needle, insert left needle tip into fronts of both slipped sts, knit both sts together from this position (decrease)

ssp . . . . [slip 1 stknitwise] twice from left needle to right needle, return both sts to left needle and purl both together through back loops

st(s) . . . . stitch(es)

St st . . . . . . stockinette stitch

tbl . . . . through back loop

tog . . . . together

W&T . . . . . wrap next stitch then turn work (often used in short rows)

WS . . . . wrong side (of work)

wyib . . . . . . with yarn in back

wyif . . . . . . with yarn in front

yb . . . . yarn back

yf . . . . yarn forward

yo . . . . yarn over

* . . . . repeat instructions from *

( ) . . . . alternate measurements and/or instructions; instructions to be worked as a group a specified number of times

Standard Yarn Weight System

Categories of yarn, gauge ranges, and recommended needle and hook sizes

Yarn Weight Symbol & Category Names	0 Lace	1 Super Fine	2 Fine	3 Light	4 Medium	5 Bulky	6 Super Bulky
Type of Yarns in Category	Fingering 10 count crochet thread	Sock, Fingering, Baby	Sport, Baby	DK, Light Worsted	Worsted, Afghan, Aran	Chunky, Craft, Rug	Bulky, Roving
Knit Gauge Range* in Stockinette Stitch to 4 inches	33 –40** sts	27–32 sts	23–26 sts	21–24 sts	16–20 sts	12–15 sts	6–11 sts
Recommended Needle in Metric Size Range	1.5–2.25 mm	2.25–3.25 mm	3.25–3.75 mm	3.75–4.5 mm	4.5–5.5 mm	5.5–8 mm	8 mm and larger
Recommended Needle U.S. Size Range	000 to 1	1 to 3	3 to 5	5 to 7	7 to 9	9 to 11	11 and larger
Crochet Gauge* Ranges in Single Crochet to 4 inch	32-42 double crochets**	21–32 sts	16–20 sts	12–17 sts	11–14 sts	8–11 sts	5–9 sts
Recommended Hook in Metric Size Range	Steel*** 1.6-1.4mm Regular hook 2.25 mm	2.25–3.5 mm	3.5–4.5 mm	4.5–5.5 mm	5.5–6.5 mm	6.5–9 mm	9 mm and larger
Recommended Hook U.S. Size Range	Steel*** 6, 7, 8 Regular hook B–1	B–1 to E–4	E–4 to 7	7 to I–9	I–9 to K–10½	K–10½ to M–13	M–13 and larger

* GUIDELINES ONLY: The above reflect the most commonly used gauges and needle or hook sizes for specific yarn categories.

** Lace weight yarns are usually knitted or crocheted on larger needles and hooks to create lacy, openwork patterns. Accordingly, a gauge range is difficult to determine. Always follow the gauge stated in your pattern.

*** Steel crochet hooks are sized differently from regular hooks--the higher the number, the smaller the hook, which is the reverse of regular hook sizing.

This Standards & Guidelines booklet and downloadable symbol artwork are available at: **YarnStandards.com**

Special Techniques Used

Applied I-cord
With double-pointed needles, CO 3 stitches in MC. K2, k2tog-tbl (attaching MC I-cord to edge st from pick-up), repeat along edge to end, k3tog.

Continental Cast-On (or Long-Tail Cast-On)
Leaving a long tail, make a slipknot and secure. Holding the needle in your right hand and the yarn in front, wrap strand counterclockwise around your left thumb with the tail over your index finger and loosely between two fingers. To make the stitch, slip the tip of the needle under the thread that is attached to the ball. Stretch the needle back over the other strands and behind the long tail. Slip the needle under the long tail thread and through the loop that is around the front of your thumb. The final step is to slide the loop off your left thumb and pull thread so that the loop holds on to the needle. Repeat this procedure until you have desired number of stitches cast-on.

Crochet Cast-On (use as Provisional Cast-On)
With waste yarn make a slip stitch and place it on a crochet hook. Put the waste yarn behind the knitting needle and hook it with the crochet hook. Use the hook to pull a new loop through the loop already on the hook. Repeat these two steps until there are enough stitches on the needle. Enlarge the last loop on the crochet hook until it is about 4"/10cm long, then cut the yarn at the top of the loop and pull out the yarn attached to the ball, being careful not to pull the remaining tail, which will be removed later.

Crochet Picot Bind-Off
With crochet hook in right hand and needle in left hand, *using crochet hook, BO 4 stitches, chain 3; repeat from * around.

Fulling (or felting)
Place knitted piece in a washing machine with a pair of jeans (or something else that will provide friction but no lint) on a hot wash cycle. Keep resetting the length of the wash cycle until the desired size is obtained. Remove before the spin cycle, rinse in cold water, shape, and air dry.

Kitchener Stitch
Place the stitches that are to be joined on two needles with needle points facing to the right. Hold needles parallel, with wrong sides together. Thread a tapestry needle with your yarn.

1. Front needle: slip the first st as if to k off the needle and go into next st on front needle as if to p and leave it on the needle, pull through both sts.
2. Back needle: slip the first st as if to p off the needle and go into next st on back needle as if to k and leave it on the needle, pull through both sts.

Repeat steps 1 and 2 for all sts on both needles. Remember to keep the working yarn beneath the needles when going from needle to needle.

Three-Needle Bind-Off
With RS's together and needles parallel, using a third needle, knit together a stitch from the front needle and a stitch from the back. *Knit together a stitch from the front and back needles and slip the first stitch over the second stitch to bind off. Repeat from * across, then fasten off last stitch.

Twined Knitting
See Twined-Knitting Technique, pages 88–89.

Unattached I-cord
With double-pointed needles *K3, do not turn work, place right needle in left hand and slip stitches to other end of double-pointed needle, wrap yarn around back of work, and repeat from * until desired length.

Twisted Cord Directions

Figure 1

Figure 2

Figure 3

Figure 4

Figure 5

Figure 6

Step 1: Measure around all four sides of the finished pillow.

Step 2: Multiply total circumference by 5 to get the length to cut your yarn for the cord. Cut the number of strands you will use and knot them together. *Note: These will be very long strands of yarn, but the length will shorten considerably as the strands are twisted; it's also better to have too much and cut the finished cord than have too little and not have enough cord to fit around the edge of the pillow.*

Step 3: Work as a team of two or find a stationary object to which to anchor one end of the knotted yarn—a doorknob is good. *(See Figure 1.)* If working in a pair, each person should hold one end of the knotted yarn, stand far enough apart that the yarn is taut but not tight, then twist counterclockwise. If the yarn is tied to a stationary object, stand back from the door so that the yarn is taut but not tight, and twist counterclockwise. *(See Figure 2.)*

Step 4: Continue twisting until the yarn twists back on itself when you give it some slack. *(See Figure 3.)*

Step 5: Fold twisted cord in half. This can be tricky, and it is especially helpful to have another set of hands so the cord doesn't become a twisted mess. *(See Figure 4.)*

Step 6: Hold on to the original two ends opposite the fold in the cord. Then let go of the rest of the cord and let it twist on itself. *(See Figure 5.)*

Step 7: Straighten out and untangle any knots. *(See Figure 6.)*

Step 8: Tie a knot in the end opposite the fold. You will tie it like the end of a balloon—an overhand knot. *(See Figures 7 and 8.)*

Step 9: Finished knot. *(See Figure 9.)*

Figure 7

Figure 8

Figure 9

Knitting References

Dandanell, Birgitta, and Ulla Dainelson. *Twined Knitting*, Loveland, CO: Interweave Press, 1989.

Gottfridsson, Inger, and Ingrid Gottfridsson. *The Mitten Book: Delightful Swedish Country Mitten Patterns with Traditional Patterns to Use for All Your Hand Knitting or Machine Knitting Projects,* Asheville, NC: Lark Books, 1987.

Ling, Anne-Maj. *Two-End Knitting*, Pittsville, WI: Schoolhouse Press, 2002.

Nylén, Anna-Maja. *Swedish Handcraft,* New York: Van Norstand Reinhold, 1977.

Solkalski, Linda. "Swedish Two-Stranded Knitting," *Threads Magazine,* No. 26 (1990): 41-48.

Solkalski, Linda. "Colorful Tvåändsstickning," *Threads Magazine,* No. 27 (1990): 68-71.

Johnson, Wendy J., and Susanna Hansson. *Bohus Stickning, Radiant Knits: An Enchanting Obsession*, Minneapolis, MN: One of Susannas and Saga Hill Designs, 2009.

Yarn Sources

Blackberry Ridge Wollen Mill
www.blackberry-ridge.com

Cascade Yarns
www.cascadeyarns.com

Louet North America
www.louet.com

JCA, Inc.
www.jcacrafts.com

Hand-Dyed Montana Merino
Ewetopia Fiber Shop
www.ewetopiafibershop.com

Lazy Susan "Yarn Buddy"
www.sunvalleyfibers.blogspot.com

Acknowledgments

We are grateful to the staff at the American Swedish Institute for allowing us access to their extensive collection. Over the past two years, we researched artifact history and took study photographs as we gathered ideas for projects. Although the institute's collection of knitted items was somewhat limited, many other artifacts, textiles and otherwise, provided inspiration for the projects in this book. In fact, it was the building itself that inspired the Mansion Mittens and the Manly Mansion Muffler.

Special thanks go to Curt Pederson, Curator at ASI, who provided many hours of assistance with artifacts, photos, history, and other last-minute requests. It was a pleasure working with someone so dedicated to cultural preservation. Thanks also to Nina Clark who supported the project from the very beginning. Nina and Curt's forward contributes an informative look at the history and culture of ASI. The volunteers at ASI are absolutely wonderful! An extra thanks to Phyllis Waggoner, who selflessly shared her extensive knowledge of Hilma Berglund. She was able to condense numerous photos and journals into a wonderful account of Hilma's contribution to the fiber arts.

We would be lost without our contributor Kate Martinson and her best friend, Harly Refsal. Thank you both for sharing your extensive knowledge of nålbindning, the Sami people, and the Dala horse as interesting sidebar information.

We'd like to extend a special thank you to the ladies in the needlework department at Ingebretsen's Scandinavian Gifts; they have been especially good to us. For several months after our first book, *Norwegian Handknits*, was released, they were generous enough to display the book and samples of the patterns at their checkout counter. It was the great success of *Norwegian Handknits* that made it possible for us to publish *Swedish Handknits*.

Many thanks to our photography sites—Gämmelgarden Museum and Pioneer Park—who granted us access to their buildings and artifacts for authentic backdrops. Also thanks to Alice Flanders, who photographed the step-by-step twined knitting how-to section. It must have been annoying to drop everything to take some shots as each technique section developed over the two weeks of knitting the Christmas sock. Alice, thanks also for modeling the sweaters at Gämmelgarden Museum.

I would also like to thank my dad, Jack Klein. Whether in woodworking or engineering, his passion for creative problem-solving skills rubbed off on me. These skills were extremely helpful in designing, especially the immigrant hood shaping. *–Sue*

Index